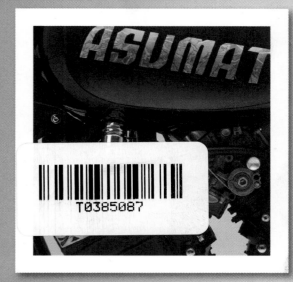

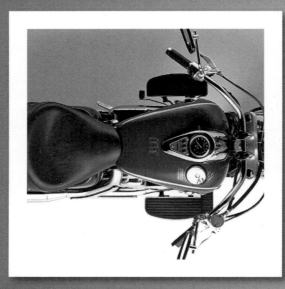

JAPANESE
CUSTOM MOTORCYCLES

**The Nippon Chop –
Chopper, Cruiser,
Bobber, Trikes &
Quads**

MOTORCYCLE-RELATED BOOKS FROM *VELOCE PUBLISHING* –

Speedpro Series
Harley-Davidson Evolution Engines, How to Build & Power Tune (Hammill)
Motorcycle-engined Racing Car, How to Build (Pashley)
Secrets of Speed – Today's techniques for 4-stroke engine blueprinting & tuning (Swager)

RAC handbooks
Caring for your bicycle – How to maintain & repair your bicycle (Henshaw)
How your motorcycle works – Your guide to the components & systems of modern motorcycles (Henshaw)
Caring for your scooter – How to maintain & service your 49cc to 125cc twist & go scooter (Fry)
Motorcycles – A first-time-buyer's guide (Henshaw)

Enthusiast's Restoration Manual Series
Classic Large Frame Vespa Scooters, How to Restore (Paxton)
Classic Smallframe Vespa Scooters, How to Restore (Paxton)
Ducati Bevel Twins 1971 to 1986 (Falloon)
Yamaha FS1-E, How to Restore (Watts)

Essential Buyer's Guide Series
BMW GS (Henshaw)
BSA 500 & 650 Twins (Henshaw)
BSA Bantam (Henshaw)
Ducati Bevel Twins (Falloon)
Ducati Desmodue Twins (Falloon)
Ducati Desmoquattro Twins - 851, 888, 916, 996, 998, ST4 1988 to 2004 (Falloon)
Harley-Davidson Big Twins (Henshaw)
Hinckley Triumph triples & fours 750, 900, 955, 1000, 1050, 1200 – 1991-2009 (Henshaw)
Honda CBR FireBlade (Henshaw)
Honda CBR600 Hurricane (Henshaw)
Honda SOHC Fours 1969-1984 (Henshaw)
Kawasaki Z1 & Z900 (Orritt)
Norton Commando (Henshaw)
Triumph Bonneville (Henshaw)
Triumph Thunderbird, Trophy & Tiger (Henshaw)
Vespa Scooters – Classic 2-stroke models 1960-2008 (Paxton)

Those Were The Days ... Series
British Drag Racing – The early years (Pettitt)
Café Racer Phenomenon, The (Walker)
Drag Bike Racing in Britain – From the mid '60s to the mid '80s (Lee)
Hot Rod & Stock Car Racing in Britain in the 1980s (Neil)
Three Wheelers (Bobbitt)

Biographies
Edward Turner – The Man Behind the Motorcycles (Clew)
Jim Redman – 6 Times World Motorcycle Champion: The Autobiography (Redman)

General
BMW Boxer Twins 1970-1995 Bible, The (Falloon)
BMW Café Racers (Cloesen)
BMW Custom Motorcycles – Choppers, Cruisers, Bobbers, Trikes & Quads (Cloesen)
Bonjour – Is this Italy? (Turner)
British 250cc Racing Motorcycles (Pereira)
BSA Bantam Bible, The (Henshaw)
BSA Motorcycles – The final evolution (Jones)
Ducati 750 Bible, The (Falloon)
Ducati 750 SS 'round-case' 1974, The Book of the (Falloon)
Ducati 860, 900 and Mille Bible, The (Falloon)
Ducati Monster Bible, The (Falloon)
Fine Art of the Motorcycle Engine, The (Peirce)
Funky Mopeds (Skelton)
Italian Custom Motorcycles (Cloesen)
Kawasaki Triples Bible, The (Walker)
Lambretta Bible, The (Davies)
Laverda Twins & Triples Bible 1968-1986 (Falloon)
little book of trikes, the (Quellin)
Moto Guzzi Sport & Le Mans Bible, The (Falloon)
Motorcycle Apprentice (Cakebread)
Motorcycle GP Racing in the 1960s (Pereira)
Motorcycle Road & Racing Chassis Designs (Noakes)
MV Agusta Fours, The book of the classic (Falloon)
Off-Road Giants! (Volume 1) – Heroes of 1960s Motorcycle Sport (Westlake)
Off-Road Giants! (Volume 2) – Heroes of 1960s Motorcycle Sport (Westlake)
Scooters & Microcars, The A-Z of Popular (Dan)
Scooter Lifestyle (Grainger)
SCOOTER MANIA! – Recollections of the Isle of Man International Scooter Rally (Jackson)
Singer Story: Cars, Commercial Vehicles, Bicycles & Motorcycle (Atkinson)
Triumph Bonneville Bible (59-83) (Henshaw)
Triumph Bonneville!, Save the – The inside story of the Meriden Workers' Co-op (Rosamond)
Triumph Motorcycles & the Meriden Factory (Hancox)
Triumph Speed Twin & Thunderbird Bible (Woolridge)
Triumph Tiger Cub Bible (Estall)
Triumph Trophy Bible (Woolridge)
Velocette Motorcycles – MSS to Thruxton – New Third Edition (Burris)

www.veloce.co.uk

For post publication news, updates and amendments relating to this book please visit www.veloce.co.uk/book/V4530

First published in December 2013 by Veloce Publishing Limited, Veloce House, Parkway Farm Business Park, Middle Farm Way, Poundbury, Dorchester, Dorset, DT1 3AR, England.
Fax 01305 250479/e-mail info@veloce.co.uk/web www.veloce.co.uk or www.velocebooks.com.
ISBN: 978-1-845845-30-8 UPC: 6-36847-04530-2

Readers with ideas for automotive books, or books on other transport or related hobby subjects, are invited to write to the editorial director of Veloce Publishing at the above address.
British Library Cataloguing in Publication Data – A catalogue record for this book is available from the British Library.
Typesetting, design and page make-up all by Veloce Publishing Ltd on Apple Mac. Printed in India by Replika Press.

JAPANESE
CUSTOM MOTORCYCLES

The Nippon Chop –
Chopper, Cruiser,
Bobber, Trikes &
Quads

Uli Cloesen

Contents

Foreword

For me, entering the world of Japanese motorcycles meant buying a Yamaha RD250 two-stroke in the mid '70s. I felt like a king in my red and black leather suit, blasting around the hills after work in South West Germany, where I grew up.

Soon realising that always being at full throttle wasn't what I wanted long-term, my next bike was a Kawasaki Z440 Ltd twin. This soft chopper, with a more relaxed four-stroke engine, good looks, and great sound and torque, made for a better suited relationship. The bike was even a reliable companion for touring duties around Europe.

The late '80s saw me purchase a Yamaha SR500;

a bestseller in Germany for many years. Lastly, Yamaha's XV750 in late 2000 rounded up all things from the land of the rising sun to date.

Converting standard motorcycles into custom bikes has always intrigued me, and this book (my fourth on the subject) reflects this. The growing trend of customising metric bikes into choppers, bobbers et al – be they high-end customs, home-built beauties, or modified late-model Japanese cruisers – is presented herein, with examples drawn from around the globe. Names like Shadow, Vulcan, Intruder and Virago conjure up images of Japanese V-twin cruisers and specials based on them, but there is much more to it. Anything can be chopped, bobbed, triked, or even turned into a street quad.

So, from singles, twins, triples, fours and sixes, experience the custom side of Japanese motorcycles.

Uli Cloesen

Introduction

Life would be boring without a touch of individuality, creativity and flair. This applies even more so to two-, three- or four-wheeled modes of transport. There has to be an emotional response, a feel-good trigger that engages us to build, ride or drive.

So, what triggered the invention of the 'bobber?' When US soldiers returned home after World War II, they wanted bikes more like the European ones they'd seen; motorcycles with less bulk than the homegrown varieties available. A bobber was created from a standard bike by 'bobbing,' or shedding weight, which usually involved scrapping the front fender and shortening the rear fender, with the intention of making a bike lighter and faster [NB: Not all countries allow the removal of fenders on bikes]. The look of a more minimalist design was also preferred to that of standard machines.

It wasn't until 1969, when American road movie *Easy Rider*, starring Peter Fonda, Dennis Hopper and Jack Nicholson, appeared that the term 'chopper' arrived on the scene. Motorcycle enthusiasts were inspired to modify their bikes in new ways, and began changing the angle of the front fork, reducing the size of the fuel tank, and adding ape hanger handlebars. To round it off, a slim front wheel and a fat rear tyre were added to the package.

The main difference between bobber and chopper bikes is that bobbers are usually built around standard frames, while chopper frames are often cut and welded to suit. Bobbers also often lack chrome parts and long forks.

A 'cruiser' is a bike created in the style of American machines from the likes of Harley-Davidson or Indian. This segment of the motorcycle market is most popular in the US. The Big Four bike manufacturers (Honda, Kawasaki, Suzuki and Yamaha) all produced V-twin cruisers for this very important market.

The riding style on a cruiser typically entails a feet-forward position with an upright body. The low-slung design of this type of bike limits its cornering ability, and chopper motorcycles are considered cruisers in this context.

A 'trike' is in essence a three-wheeled motorcycle, carrying its rider and up to two passengers, depending on specification. For those who don't like the idea of riding a bike, but seek the same thrill of acceleration and speed, a trike which has the added safety of an extra wheel, could be the answer. In many countries you don't have to wear a helmet when riding a trike, because they can be registered like a car.

The 'quad' was introduced about three decades ago with the Honda US 90 – the first all-terrain vehicle (ATV). Less expensive to run and smaller and more manoeuvrable than a ute or tractor, with low-pressure tyres suited to soft ground, ATVs became essential on farms, and even as a means of mobility for the disabled. A new breed of quad has since evolved for road use, with high-performance engines and car-type chassis, and it's these that feature in this book.

Lastly, for any metric conversion needs, refer to www.metric-conversions.org.

ACKNOWLEDGEMENTS

The author and publisher wish to acknowledge their debt to all who loaned material and photographs for this book. Thank you also to Honda, Kawasaki, Suzuki, and Yamaha for providing material.

You are welcome to contact us to have your Japanese-powered Chopper, Cruiser, Bobber, Trike or Quad considered for an updated edition of this book in the future.

CHAPTER 1
HONDA

onda has built a fine heritage of custom-style motorcycles over the years. The company's first V-twin bike, the Honda CX500, dates back to 1978, and its custom variant, the CX500C, was released in 1979. The model was restyled in 1983, and engine capacity was increased to 673cc.

The transversely-mounted, 500cc, liquid-cooled V-twin, featuring a pushrod actuated four-valve head and shaft drive. (Courtesy Rose Rosan)

The VT600/VLX features a 583cc, V-twin engine, four-speed transmission, chain drive, and a single-shock softail-style rear suspension. The 2003 version is shown here. (Courtesy Honda)

CX650 CUSTOM 1983

The CX variants set the stage for Honda's long line of factory-made cruisers. This is a restyled 1983 CX650 model. (Courtesy Honda)

2009 VTX1300C. (Courtesy Honda)

HONDA SHADOW

1983 also marked the introduction of the Honda Shadow line of cruiser motorcycles. These were powered by a liquid-cooled, 52-degree V-twin engine with a displacement of 125 to 1800cc, at a time when custom styling cues such as teardrop tanks, pull back handlebars, stepped seats and chrome parts were very fashionable. The Honda 250cc Rebel is sold under the Shadow label in some markets.

The first Shadow models were the VT500C and VT750C. The VT750C was reduced to 699cc in 1984 when tariff restrictions were imposed on Japanese bikes over 750cc imported to the US. The tariff was lifted in 1985, which resulted in the release of the VT1100C.

In 1988 the VT750C's capacity was increased to 800cc, with the model designation VT800C.

The VT600C, also known as the Honda Shadow VLX, was launched

Shadow Spirit. (Courtesy Honda)

Shadow Aero. (Courtesy Honda)

Shadow Phantom, with its factory bobber-style. (Courtesy Honda)

the same year. Designed to be an entry-level Shadow model, the motor was taken from the Honda Transalp.

The Shadow line changed little until 1997, when the Shadow Ace 750 was introduced.

The Honda Shadow Sabre replaced the VT1100 model in 2000, before the 1100cc line gave way to the new VTX1300 in 2007.

Inspiration for the VTX models stemmed from the Zodia concept bike unveiled at the Tokyo Motor Show in 1995.

In 2002 Honda released a VTX1800 V-twin, which was the largest production V-twin on the market. A 1300cc version followed suit in 2003.

In 2011 the Shadow line was limited to four 750cc variants. Pictures of 2012 models follow.

Italian designer Luca Bar's idea of a VT750RS Shadow Scrambler.

Shadow RS, which can be seen as the Honda Sportster, to name its direct competitor, the Harley Sportster. (Courtesy Honda)

MUGEN MRV 1000

Hirotoshi Honda's company, Mugen, built this beautiful 1000cc V-twin.

JAPANESE CUSTOM MOTORCYCLES

TECHNICAL DATA

Engine	Air-cooled, four-stroke, OHV3VLV V-twin, two-cylinder
Displacement.	995cc
Max Ps	51.2Ps (37.7kw) / 5000rpm
Max torq. (kg-m/rpm). .	8.1kg-m (79.43Nm) / 3000rpm
Bore x stroke	89.0 x 80.0mm
Compression ratio.	9.0:1
Dimensions (L x W x H) ..	2264 x 665 x 1121mm
Wheelbase	1552mm
Dry weight..	191kg
Front brake	Oil-pressurised inboard braking system
Rear brake.	Mechanical dual leading drum brake
Frame	Semi-double cradle-type

Above & below: This bike was conceived by Soichiro Honda's son in the classic Brit bike mold. The Mugen MRV 1000 from the '80s gives a roadster nod to the past.
This model would have been costly to manufacture in series production, so only one complete bike was built.
(Courtesy Mugen/M-Tec)

Honda Magna

The Honda Magna cruiser was produced from 1982-1988, and again from 1994-2003. The V4 engine, with its 90-degree layout, was taken from VF/VFR models. Its four-cylinder powertrain ran much smoother than a V-twin, and the short-stroke and large piston diameter enabled a high redline and top speed.

The Magna line came in 500cc (V30), 750cc (V45) and 1100cc (V65) displacements. A 250cc (V25) entry-level version was also produced from 1994-2003.

A 1995 V45. Performance of the V45 was comparable to Honda's Valkyrie six-cylinder and 1800cc Shadow cruisers. (Courtesy Honda)

Honda Gold Wing Cruisers/Concepts

The 1520cc (93in³) Honda Valkyrie was a cruiser derived from the Gold Wing tourer, and built 1997-2003. The model was coded GL1500C in the US and F6C in other countries. The Valkyrie was manufactured in the US at the Honda motorcycle plant in Marysville, Ohio.

Prior to the release of its Rune production motorcycle, Honda presented four concept bikes based on the Gold Wing's horizontally opposed six-cylinder engine, coded T1-T4 (the T4 concept from 2000 is pictured).

The Valkyrie Rune was a major departure from the original Valkyrie cruiser in terms of styling and purpose. Introduced in 2003 as a limited edition model, it used the 1832cc (111.8in³) Gold Wing engine.

Single-seat Valkyrie with Ray Gun-style end cans. (Courtesy Bob Mallett)

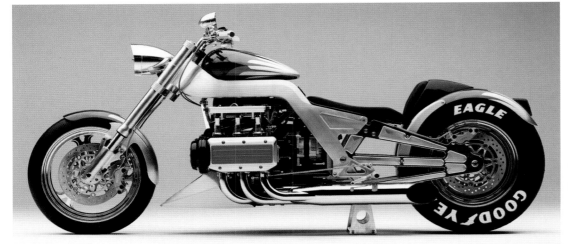

T4 Valkyrie-based concept drag bike. (Courtesy Honda)

TECHNICAL DATA – HONDA RUNE

Model	NRX1800
Engine	1832cc, liquid-cooled, horizontally opposed, six-cylinder
Bore x stroke	74 x 71mm
Compression ratio	9.8:1
Valve train	SOHC; two valves per cylinder
Carburation	PGM-FI with automatic choke
Ignition	Computer-controlled digital with three-dimensional mapping
Transmission	Five-speed
Final drive	Shaft
Front suspension	Trailing-link; 3.9in of travel
Rear suspension	Unit Pro-Link with single shock; 3.9in of travel
Front brake	Dual, full-floating 330mm discs with three piston callipers
Rear brake	Single, 336mm disc with two-piston calliper
Front tyre	150/60R-18 radial
Rear tyre	180/55R-17 radial
Wheelbase	68.9in
Seat height	27.2in
Dry weight	794lb
Fuel capacity	6.1 gallons
Colours	Illusion Blue, Double Clear Coat Black, Candy Black Cherry

California version differed slightly due to emissions equipment.

Honda produced this trimmed-down Bagger-styled Gold Wing F6B in 2013.

Honda's EVO6 concept motorcycle was unveiled at the 2007 Tokyo Motor Show, and was also based on the flat-six, 1832cc engine.

The EVO6 features a Human Friendly Transmission (HFT) that's operated in fully automatic or six-speed manual mode. (Courtesy Sacha Padovani)

The Rune features a trailing-link front suspension and single-side swingarm. (Courtesy Honda)

EVO6 rear view. (Courtesy Evan Hayden)

HONDA FURY

Honda introduced the Fury in May 2009, and it was designed in the US to appeal to the custom chopper market.

Features such as the tall steering head giving the frame a see-through, open-air look and the sculpted fuel tank sitting high atop the frame's backbone helped give the bike that distinct chopper stance. The 1312cc (80.1in³) V-twin engine was derived from Honda's VTX1300 cruiser model.

Engineering the liquid-cooled motor so that its 'plumbing' always looked clean was no easy task. Honda packaged the unobtrusive radiator neatly between the frame's dual down tubes, and the radiator hose leading to the forward cylinder was cleverly concealed beneath the valve cover.

The nine-spoke front wheel looks great; especially the right side where it's not obstructed by a brake disc. The driveshaft to the rear wheel is mated to the five-speed transmission. (Courtesy Honda)

TECHNICAL DATA

Model	VT1300CXA
Engine	Liquid-cooled, SOHC, 52°, V-twin
Displacement	1312cc
Bore x stroke	89.5 x 104.3mm
Compression ratio	9.2:1
Max torque	107Nm / 2250min-1
Carburation	PGM-FI with automatic enricher circuit
Throttle bore	40mm
Fuel tank capacity	12.8 litres
Ignition system	Digital with 3-dimensional mapping, 2 sparkplugs per cylinder
Starter	Electric
Transmission	5-speed
Final drive	Enclosed shaft drive
Frame	Double-cradle; steel
Dimensions (L x W x H) . .	2575 x 900 x 1150mm
Wheelbase	1805mm
Caster angle	32° (offset to 38° effect)
Trail	92mm
Seat height	685mm
Ground clearance	125mm
Kerb weight	309kg all standard equipment, required fluids and a full tank of fuel – ready to ride
Front suspension	45mm telescopic fork with 102mm axle travel
Rear suspension	Mono shock with adjustable rebound damping and 35-position spring preload adjustability, 95mm axle travel
Wheels	9-spoke cast front and rear
Tyres	Front: 90/90-21 Rear: 200/50-18
Front brake	ABS 336mm single disc with twin-piston calliper
Rear brake	ABS, 296mm disc with single-piston calliper

HONDA CRUISERS

Honda's new-for-2010 Interstate, Sabre, and Stateline offered new twists on the factory custom cruiser theme.

The Interstate is the longer-distance bike; with floorboards, saddlebags and a windscreen.

The Stateline cruiser uses the same 1312cc V-twin, and the single-pin power plant (as opposed to the dual-pin setup found in the VTX1800) creates a pleasant pulse that is common with Harley engines.

2012 Stateline. (Courtesy Honda)

2012 Interstate. (Courtesy Honda)

HONDA CONCEPT BIKES

In an effort to show how the firm's latest cruisers could be customised, the US R&D arm of Honda revealed three concept bikes in 2010 that were based on its VT1300 range.

Fury 'Furious'

Based on the 2010 Fury, the long and low 'Furious' (Hardtail Chopper) was created by Nick Renner to have a blend of new and old-school looks. The bike features a 23in wheel up front and a 20in on the rear. A 45-degree rake and converted hardtail create a clean chopper stance.

2010 Fury 'Furious.' (Courtesy Honda)

SPECIFICATION

- Stock VT1300cc engine & tank
- 23in front wheel, 20in rear
- Exposed shaft drive
- Hardtail custom spec frame conversion (37° head pipe with an 8° fork angle offset)
- Custom oversize drag bars, custom paint
- Straight pipe exhaust
- Custom diamond-stitched leather seat & rear hugger

Metal flake and a diamond-stitched seat contrast with the five-spoke wheels and Fury tank. (Courtesy Honda)

Sabre 'Switchblade' (Pro Drag)

Designer Edward Birtulescu conceived the Switchblade, using the 2010 Sabre as its base. The main focus of the design was speed, emphasised by features such as a full carbon fibre dress, racing 3-way adjustable suspension, and a single-sided swingarm with a 535 chain conversion.

Sabre 'Switchblade.' (Courtesy Honda)

SPECIFICATION

- Stock frame, VT1300cc engine, and tank
- 3-way fully adjustable sport suspension
- Carbon fibre custom bodywork & special seat
- 535 chain conversion (before shaft drive)
- Single-sided swingarm conversion
- Racing spec callipers & discs
- Carbon fibre 18in rear wheel & 21in front
- Onboard GPS lap timer & data acquisition unit
- Oversized billet top and lower bridge
- Air box/cleaner conversion

Stateline 'Slammer' (Bagger)

Designer Erik Dunshee based the 'Slammer' on a 2010 Stateline. It sports fully adjustable air-ride suspension and Nav Multimedia head unit with 10in subwoofer and 500W power. Dunshee achieved a full front end conversion, including a lean 23in custom wheel, without frame or engine modification.

SPECIFICATION

- Stock frame, swingarm, VT1300cc engine, and tank
- 23in specially-designed front wheel
- Fully 'air-ride adjustable' front & rear suspension, 6in ride height to 2.25in lowered
- Composite coated narrow track front disc with 6-piston calliper
- Nav Multimedia head unit with GPS speed display
- 3-speaker (including a 10in subwoofer) 500W sound system
- Full custom bodywork, including a leather drop seat
- Two-tone Satin Metallic Black & Pearl Black paint
- Custom spec crossover twin-pipe exhaust
- Air-box/cleaner conversion

Custom bikes come in all shapes and sizes; it really depends on the builder's vision and taste. The rest of this chapter explores some of these Honda-based customs, from single-cylinder motorcycles, through twins, fours and sixes, to trikes and quads.

DARIZT DESIGN, INDONESIA

Custom builder Agus Darizt operates Darizt Design from a small home garage in Jogja, a little city in the center of Java, Indonesia.

Agus: "Here in Indonesia we have a limited selection of bikes, resources, and tools, from which I try to create something else, something different.

"Creating custom bikes mainly involves only myself, but my brothers also help with some of the preparation and research. I prefer to build bikes one at a time, so I can be more focused and feel more integrated with the project. All of my previous jobs involved drawing, from book illustrator, painter, statue maker, model maker, interior designer to airbrush artist. Combine this with my obsession for motorcycles, and my head is always full of imagination for building custom bikes.

"I began making custom bikes from scale model kits, because I couldn't afford the real thing.

"My job as an airbrush artist working on custom build Harleys put me on the path to becoming a bike builder, but it wasn't until an old friend of mine got in touch that it really began.

"Three years ago, just as my dream of building bikes had started to fade, my friend convinced me to build a bike for him from scratch.

**Stateline 'Slammer.'
(Courtesy Honda)**

The Preambule; based on a '76 CB100. (Courtesy Sony)

I learnt how to weld, how to use a bench lathe machine, and refine my metal shaping techniques, and five months later the Preambule (orange CB100) was finished.

"As a junk collector, inspiration comes from everything around me in my daily life, and sometimes I visited junk yards, flea markets, or a hardware store thinking 'what if I put this thing on a bike ...'"

SPECIFICATION

- The engine is the only item that remains from the donor CB bike
- The cylinder head and carb were replaced with those from a GL200, along with other parts, to boost performance
- Frame, front suspension and handlebar were made from seamless steel tube, with old-fashioned bending tools.
- Fuel tank, exhaust pipe, forward control, saddle, lamps, and other accessories were handmade from metal/sheet metal
- Tyres and wheels are 21in, front and rear. Wheel hubs and discs are from a Gas-Gas trial bike
- Paintwork completed in-house (in the garage), except for the engine and exhaust that required powder coating

Darizt Design – the '2nd project' ('85 GL100)

SPECIFICATION

- The frame, front & rear suspension, and handlebar are made from steel tube
- The fuel tank, exhaust pipe, forward controls, saddle, lamps and other accessories were handmade from metal/sheet
- Some parts were taken from a bicycle, like the seat cover, seat post, cable adjuster, etc

The tyres and wheels are 19in, the front drum brake is from a Yamaha DT, and the rear left-sided drum brake is custom-made from Piaggio Vespa drum brake parts.

Unlike the Preambule, there was no special treatment for this engine, only a small ignition and wiring upgrade. (Courtesy Adhe)

Darizt Design – the '4th project'

This bike is based on a '70 Honda CB200. (Courtesy Sony)

As with other Darizt bikes, almost all of the components are handmade, some sourced from local bikes and some even bicycle parts.

SPECIFICATION
- The tyres are 19-3.50 with 19in 1.60 wheels
- The front drum brake is from an old dirt bike
- The rear left-sided drum brake is custom-made with parts taken from a Piaggio Vespa's front drum brake

GENERATION Z PROJECT, MASSEY UNIVERSITY, NEW ZEALAND

The static bike model pictured right was spotted in an exhibition during the opening of the Creative Arts Building on the Wellington campus of Massey University in June 2012.

The project evolved through collaboration between Massey University senior industrial designer Oliver Neuland and Honda Europe chief designer Paolo Cuccagna, with the aim of designing a road bike that would appeal to young adults.

Cuccagna visited industrial design students at Massey's Wellington and Albany campuses to set up a design competition for them. After selecting one of 24 concepts submitted, a group of eight students from the Albany School of Design were supplied with a Honda CBR125 to use as a foundation and template for a full-size clay model of the chosen entry.

It will be interesting to see what influence this project has on Honda's plans for attracting Generation Z into its fold.

The Generation Z project on display. (Author collection)

Initial concept sketches by Sam McCafferty.

Two Honda twin-cylinder-based customs ...

ROB LEE, NEW ZEALAND

Rob's customised Honda began life as a pink rolling frame and three boxes of random parts, which he bought on the Kiwi biker Forum for $250 – a fourth box of parts is still out there somewhere.

Rob: "Most of my time since then has been spent sourcing parts and grinding various bits off the frame, and messing about with stuff. It's been a big learning experience because I'm not very mechanically-minded. The bike went through various 'looks,' and still isn't finalised – are they ever?"

The CB450 bobber.

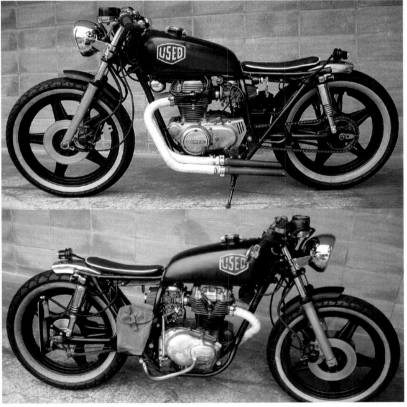

This bike began life as a 1973 Honda CB360. The logo is intended as a pun about DEUS customs.

SCOTT HALBLEIB, US

Scott has been into motorcycling for years, but had always rode modern-day machines. A visit to the local Louisville Vintage Motorworks club, which focuses on vintage Japanese and British bikes, as well as scooters, got him hooked. He'd seen their bikes in original and modified form, and was keen to build something of his own.

Scott began doing a lot of web research and stumbled upon the Japanese Gravel Crew website. He was amazed by some of its work; the lines and stances of the bikes were exactly what he was looking for.

Scott: "I perused eBay and came across a '71 CB450 in a neighbouring state. The bid was won, and I spent a few months riding the bike in stock form. But it didn't have the look I wanted, so I began deconstructing the bike.

"It had to be something a little more hot rod than shiny custom. Bobbers are hot rods in my mind, and that's what I wanted – something that would slightly bother the neighbours, but be cool enough that they'd want to let it slide.

"So while I was able to cut, grind, sand, and spray some items for the frame, handlebars, fender, and other miscellaneous items, I knew I'd need to out-source some work.

"Benjie from BCR in Edison NJ agreed to make the tank and exhaust for the project.

"Next, I asked Woody's Wheel Works to build the wheels. I supplied the tyre info and sent the stock hubs. It powder coated, laced and mounted it all, only for me to discover that I could no longer use a disc up front. So I sourced a drum brake on eBay, and the process had to be repeated.

"The passenger peg mounts were ground off the frame, the rear fender got chopped, some straight bars were fabricated, a number plate bracket added, and an old Ford tail light was incorporated. Then I had to Kwik Blast the lot for final fabrication, paint, and assembly.

"Eight months later, she returned almost complete, three days before two bike shows. Doug Devine from the vintage club spent

The bike strikes a good stance.

The new, more rounded tank was sourced from a Honda CX500C. The rear frame was removed, and a custom exhaust system and new fenders built. The battery box was moved, and a new seat unit fitted. Some Tomaselli and Tarozzi parts were fitted, with the speedometer sourced from a Mini. A metallic brown paint job finished it off. The transformed CX500 was entered into the Danish Forever Two Wheels bike show where it took the honours in the Open class – mission accomplished!

SPECIFICATION

- CX 500E frame
- CX 500C engine, tank & wheels
- Rear frame & brackets removed
- K&N filters
- Standard swingarm
- Front fork lowered
- WM custom battery box under engine
- WM custom rear fender
- WM custom seat
- Comstar 19in front and 16in rear, semi-gloss black wheels
- Firestone Deluxe tyres
- WM custom front fender
- WM custom steel windshield
- Mini speedometer
- WM custom exhaust system
- Tarozzi foot pegs
- Bitubo rear shocks
- New wiring and lights
- Secondhand rear light
- Mini headlight
- Tomaselli quick gas grip
- Tarozzi clip-ons
- Posh grips
- Brembo brake master
- Drilled front discs
- Steel braided brake hoses

three full days reworking the fuel lines and electrical system, and tweaking the carburettors for me. The bike was finished at 10pm the night before its first show, Mods vs Rockers 2010, where it won best rocker and best in show. It went on to win best Japanese bike at the Beatersville Show the same year, and again at the Indy Rockers Reunion 2011. I would like to thank all those involved in helping me build this bobber."

Next up are three examples of what can be achieved with the old Honda CX range ...

WRENCHMONKEES, DENMARK

The Wrenchmonkees workshop in Copenhagen is well-known for its custom builds. So when it was contacted by CX500 owner Max from France, inquiring about transforming his bike, the deal was on.

Wrenchmonkees decided to customise this CX500 into a chopper/racer-style bike. The frame needed some rust repairs, but the engine was in good condition, and left untouched.

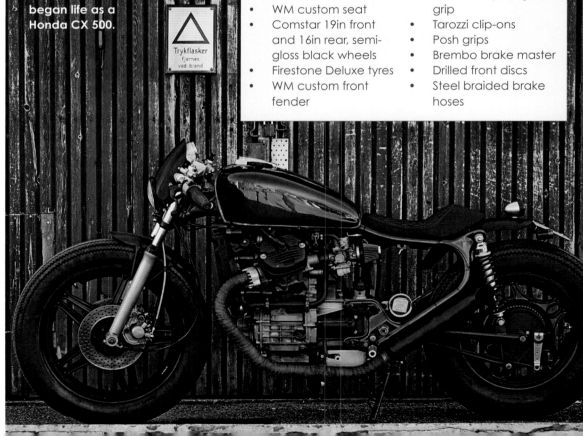

This custom began life as a Honda CX 500.

HONDA CX500
STREET-TRACKER
BY RIVE GAUCHE KUSTOMS

RIVE GAUCHE KUSTOMS
PARIS

RIVE GAUCHE KUSTOMS, FRANCE

The CX500 Street Tracker is the work of Julien and Vincent from Rive Gauche Kustoms, based in Paris.

It has been stripped back to essentials, and with the engine painted white and the rest of the bike black, it really makes a statement.

Left & above: The bike is fitted with Continental TKC 80 Twinduro tyres, 140/80-18 rear, and 110/80-19 front, made possible by replacement of the rear rim. The engine is painted in 'Old English White.'

DORIAN NAVARETTE, US

This hardtailed bobber/
chopper custom started life as
a '83 Honda CX650C.

TECHNICAL DATA

Builder/owner	Dorian Navarrete, Los Angeles, US
Displacement	650cc
Exhaust	Stock, modified
Transmission	Stock
Forks	Stock
Chassis	Stock, modified to hardtail
Suspension	Factory rebuilt front forks, rear hardtail
Fuel tank	Stock Honda p-nut
Fenders	None
Seat	Custom spring leather seat from Chris at redtailleather.com
Wheels	Stock, painted Ford Hot Rod Red
Special features	Carb velocity stacks, custom number plate, & rear 150/90/15 white sidewall tyre

TAIL END CUSTOMS, US

Josh's Texan-based company builds affordable bobbers and also offers custom parts to its clientele.

They have worked on Honda Rebels, Honda Shadow VLX600s, Yamaha V-Star 650s, Yamaha XS400s, and Yamaha XS650s. Customers usually bring their own bikes, or a donor bike is sourced for the build.

2006 Honda Shadow
VLX600 custom bobber
by Tail End Customs.

AFT Customs, US
Asumati

AFT Customs, based in Jackson California, doubles as a metric customiser and modeling agency. All the AFT Custom girls not only model but also work on the motorcycles, hence most of Asumati was completed by the AFT Custom girls. This bike was a competitor in the Freestyle class of the 2011 AMD World Championships of Custom Bike Building. The bike is fully street legal, even though all the components are custom-made.

Jim Giuffra: "This bike was commissioned by the Jackson Rancheria Hotel & Casino. It is a 'Street Tracker' design to handle the mountain roads of the Sierra Nevada mountains. This bike will be on permanent display in the casino."

SPECIFICATION
- Custom Race Tech rear shocks
- Yamaha R1 front forks
- Upswept pipe for ground clearance
- Digital lights, instruments & handlebar switches
- 1⅜in Super Moto bars (AFT was the first to use these on a custom [Kemosabe])
- AFT engine performance package
- Naked engine (AFT original)
- Removable tail section for passenger
- Hidden radiator
- Super Moto hand controls
- 420lb (wet) weight
- Number plate rotates horizontal to vertical (AFT original)
- Hand engraving

(And overleaf:) 'Asumati' is based on a Honda VT750ST, and its name is actually a Miwuk word meaning Grizzly Bear. It features beautiful detailed engraving on the cylinder heads and engine cover. **(Courtesy Mike Chase Photography)**

Green Honda bobber

Jim: "This was our first entry into the World Championships of custom bike building by AMD in 2005. It was the first year the show had a Metric class. All AFT bikes are timeless in design. This bike had a hidden radiator, suicide shift with number plate/shock and 8in headlight, all of which we pioneered.

"All AFT bikes are built by the AFT Customs Girls modelling agency. The girls are promotional models for the power sports industry, and also work on each of our builds. Collectively, the girls build about 60-70 percent of each bike under my supervision.

"They have been taught metal shaping, welding, engine building, wheel lacing, and have just completed an introduction class on air brushing. Two of the girls hold a TIG welding certification. They love building bikes. It's their hobby, and their enthusiasm has won the respect of thousands of people."

This green bobber made history in 2005 by being the first Metric World Champion of custom bike building, and it's still in style now, more than eight years later. (Courtesy Mike Chase Photography)

The bobber was also converted to belt drive. (Courtesy Mike Chase Photography)

TECHNICAL DATA – GREEN HONDA BOBBER

Performance	Horse power increased 30% from stock
Engine	Design Performance 11:1 pistons & cams, Barnett clutch
Intake	Thunder MFG air filter, Dynojet jet kit
Exhaust	Cobra/AFT Customs. Heat wrapped
Paint	Scott Hultquist/Riff Raff Customs. PPG custom mix. Frame & case covers by Mark Gallardo. Gloss Black
Chrome	Ernesto Dominguez
Powder coating	Dynamic Coatings
Polishing	AFT Customs
Seat	Duane Ballard Custom Seats
Drive	Scoot Works belt drive
Suspension	Lowered 1.5in. Rear: 11in Progressive 'FL' style shocks. Front: AFT Customs lowering kit/shaved legs
Wheels	Honda 17inx3.5 rims. Buchanan polished stainless spokes
Tyres	Michelin Macadam 130/90x17in
Frame	Stock. Rear fender struts bobbed, all unnecessary mounts, rear foot pegs, and brake stay arm removed. Cover over radiator added
AFT Customs	Radiator relocation kit, fuel tank, 8in headlight, single-pull throttle, handlebars, number plate holder, suicide shifter, turn signal mounts, carb cover, brake pedal
Arlen Ness	Mirror, radiator pipe mounts
Custom Chrome	Rear fender, tail light, mirror mount
Cobra	F. master cylinder cap
Golan Products	Fuel filter
S&S	Velocity stacks
Spiegler	Front brake hose, turn signals
Cat Eye Customs	Grips, foot pegs, brake pedal, toe piece, foot pegs shaved, raised 1in
Motion Pro	Cables
Paul Yaffe	Gas Cap
Pingel	Petcock
Kuryakyn	LED accent lights under fuel tank
Misc	Relocated: radiator, battery, fuel pump, horn, ignition switch, rectifier, starter button, idiot lights moved to triple clamp. Wiring: internal handlebar wiring with stainless covering. Stainless spark plug wires

LowLa

Jim: "LowLa was Sukhee's (AFT Girl) personal bike. It won many shows and was featured in several magazines. It took 7th at the 2009 Freestyle AMD Championship."

SPECIFICATION

- Hidden radiator
- Honda/AFT Customs front suspension. Legend Air Suspension at rear
- RC Components 'Raven' wheels; 23in front, 18in rear
- Naked Engine (AFT design)
- Top end narrowed 2in
- Pyrex coolant tube (pioneered by AFT)
- Diamond-shaped headlight
- Hydraulic clutch conversion (pioneered by AFT)
- AFT engine performance package
- Keyless remote ignition
- Lyndall composit discs
- Super bike foot controls

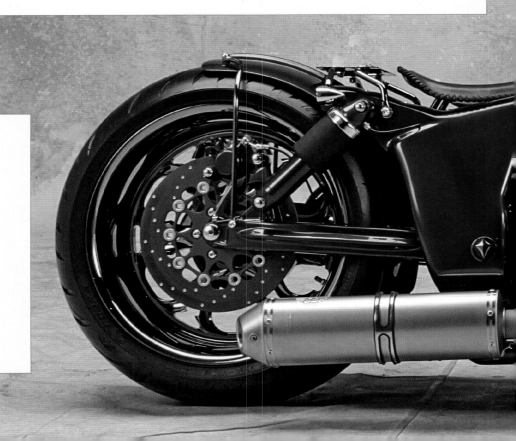

(And overleaf:) LowLa was built in 2009, and started life as a stock Honda VTX1300. It features a detachable make-up case (inset, right). (Courtesy Mike Chase Photography)

Ever since Honda's iconic CB750 appeared in 1969, its engine has remained very popular with custom bike builders. Two fine examples follow ...

Venice Choppers, US

Chris Tragert began building bikes with the resurrection of a Honda S90 in 1972, and a succession of race bikes, café racers, choppers, and custom bikes have followed.

Venice Choppers was founded in 1990, custom building bikes for use in television commercials. In addition to corporate clients, the company also offers ground-up custom builds, as well as period correct restoration of original 1970s bikes.

Venice bobber

Chris: "This bare-knuckle Venice bobber is a product of its environment. A light, compact weapon was needed to slice through the traffic-choked urban sprawl surrounding the sea-side oasis where it was conceived. Lightweight, quickness, agile handling, and good brakes were top priority. The resulting menacing appearance would give 'murderous cagers' something to text about.

"To achieve the above-mentioned criteria, an early 1970s Amen rigid frame complete with original oil tank/battery tray was used. A stock length CB750 front end, combined with a 21in rim, had the frame sitting low and level. A 17in CB750 rear wheel kept things slim; its drum brake actuated by a 40in Ford brake pedal operated from solid, mid-mount foot pegs.

"Confident the chassis was up to the task, it received a silky coat of satin black powder coat, topped with stainless steel spokes, and polished calliper, triple clamp, and rear sprocket.

"Motivation comes from a '78 CB750F motor. Stripped down, and rebuilt, with chrome covers, and stainless hardware, it breathes through early CB carbs jetted to suit the vintage Dunstall exhaust. This rare 4-2 collector is tipped with 2in exhaust cutouts. 8in baffles attach to the end caps, providing a mellow exhaust note from discreetly

The bike has a minimalist, muscular stance. Its Alien fuel tank, powder coated Charcoal Metallic with a Candy Red top coat, gives a 50+ mile range.

drilled outlets. Removing the end caps reminds the neighbours who the bad-boy on the block is. Sparking the mix are chrome Harley coils, with copper core wires, and 'Rajah' caps more commonly found on flathead Fords. Coil position mimics drag racing magnetos, in case anyone questions your intentions, which should be clear, based on the aggressive riding position.

"Clubman bars get your hunch on, while keeping your knuckles below mirror level when splitting lanes. A Hayabusa master cylinder feeds the venerable Honda disc some extra juice, in a world of ABS induced delayed reactions.

"Completing the interface of man and machine, is a West Eagle seat, sprung with 2in Bates springs. Its kicked up rear keeps yours in its place, and off the 5in rear fender.

"Spontaneous, nocturnal missions are illuminated by a Lucas driving lamp. Backup is provided by a VW turn signal, stuffed with red LEDs. Wired up, and fired up, this bike has proven to be an effective tool for traversing the urban landscape. It's lean looks are a direct result of it's dedication to function, proving less is more, and if you need more, here it is."

Venice Digger

Chris: "This Venice Chop started life with the swap meet purchase of an old Durfee girder–short and stiff. I immediately envisioned the 'digger'-style chops I remember tearing around the San Francisco bay area in the late 1970s.

A skinny 18in rear wheel and a 21in trail bike front wheel were bolted to the beefed frame; keeping things looking lean, and providing some useable stopping power.

Hustle comes from a stock CB750 motor, the flow from powder coated cases, Alphabet filters, Harley coils and a Cragar S/S points cover. Merged head pipes tuck in tight, and feed into Wassel mufflers for a mellow tone.

"Out by Redwood City, attacking the twisties on my RD350, I was passed by a strutted, low-riding Sportster. It was a particularly defining moment. I was a squid. That cat was cool.

"Redemption came over 25 years later in the form of a vintage Santee frame. It had the necessary stretch and just enough rake to achieve the long, low look I was after. It also had a cracked top tube,

and some gnarly stick welds. A new top tube was clam-shelled over the old one, and much grinding ensued.

"The prism tank was salvaged from the remains of a pink metalflake Z-1 chopper that turned up in a Penny Saver ad. Along with the custom seat, 5in fender, and one-piece pullback bars, it works to keep this modern rendition locked in the '70s.

"The frame and tin were filled with weld and ground smooth in preparation for powder coating. The colour was chosen by an informal survey. I rode the bare metal mock-up down to the Venice boardwalk, with colour chart. Of those whose opinions I admired the most, blue with silver sparkle was the unanimous choice.

"Bolted back together with stainless hardware, the finished product is light and responsive, with sleek looks. The Venice Digger has captured the qualities of the original creations that inspired it. Cool at last."

DON BRANSCOM, US

Don's custom chopper (pictured top of next page) has at its heart a Honda V4 engine, and it certainly doesn't lack power.

SPECIFICATION
- Custom-built frame made with DOM steel tubing, all TIG welded
- Hand-built 'Tractor/Pizza'-style seat
- Custom handlebars
- Rear wheel 240mm. Front wheel 21in
- Crossflow Honda V65 1100 radiator
- 4.5in ground clearance
- Some engine cases have been polished
- Build time was one year

The engine is a liquid-cooled Honda VF1000R, gear driven, DOHC V4 with 121hp. The frame has 42° rake and 4.5in trail.

Honda's Gold Wing tourer is not immune to the custom treatment either ...

KEVIN ROWLAND, US

Kevin described the Gold Wing transformation shown below as a winter project for the fun of it, that had its own challenges. The previous owner crashed the bike before storing it under a blue tarpaulin for more than twenty years.

The suspension, carburettors and brake components were corroded, but the price was right. Kevin fitted GSX-R forks and a custom mono shock, plus a pair of Weber 40 carbs from a VW, then added CBR hand controls and installed a hydraulic clutch. The tank was sourced from a CB750, supplemented by an old propane tank, which was chopped, sectioned and turned into an auxiliary. Plenty of welding, some machining, and a bunch of custom parts followed before she was again road-worthy.

Kevin: "Most people can't believe it when I tell them it's just a 1983 Honda Gold Wing. Other than cutting a few things off, the frame is stock. The carbs give it a bit of a different punch, the pipes make it sound like an angry VW, and the stance is a little more aggressive."

(And overleaf, top:) This custom started life as a 1983 GL1100. Since its resurrection it has certainly attracted lots of attention.

This bobber was based on a 1983 Honda Gold Wing Interstate.

Alloy parts were cleaned and 'rubbed' to show-off the 30-year-old patina.

RICHARD BECKER, US

Ric specialises in four-cylinder Gold Wing custom builds, and his intention for 'Ol' Sparky' was a vintage-style bobber look – an aim he's achieved rather well.

SPECIFICATION

- Original frame
- Lowered and raked 33°
- Softail pull-shock rear suspension
- Rust colour powder coat
- Fuel contained in a sectioned piece of the original wing tank plumbed in tandem with a faux oil bag (3gal total)
- 2 BBL Weber carburettor (inside fake tank) on a custom HOTT intake manifold
- Lithium-ion battery hidden between the shocks & exhaust
- All work completed in-house

BIKER'S BEST, NETHERLANDS
Gold Wing chopper

A blast from the past (story and photos courtesy of Onno Berserk Wieringa). John de Weerdt had déjà vu when he bumped into the white Gold Wing chopper pictured opposite.

More than twenty years ago, John had seen this bike on a daily basis – dragging it to fairs/shows around Europe, polishing and pampering

The white hardtail Gold Wing; a rare sight. The bike has a good stance.

Close-up of the fork and paint job.

Rear section view.

TECHNICAL DATA

Owner . . . . Biker's Best
Builder . . . . Geert Prudon
Brand. . . . . Honda
Model . . . . Hardtail Chopper

Engine block

Year of construction 1976
Capacity. 1000cc
Air filter.. . . . . Handmade
Air filter housing .. . . Handmade
Ignition.. . . . . Dyna
Exhaust system . . . . Square dragpipes

Gearbox

Year of construction 1976
Final transmission .. . . . . Shaft drive

Frame

Year of construction 1977
Type . . . . Hardtail
Builder .. . . Geert Prudon
Stretch.. . . . . 6in
Shock absorbers.. . . . . . None
Fork . . . . Girder

Wheels, brakes & tyres

Front wheel .. . . Custom
  Type . . . . Spaak wheel
  Size 4x16in
  Brakes. . . . . Girder-type
  Tyres . . . . Continental
Rear wheel. . . . . Custom, with Honda hub
  Type . . . . Spaak wheel
  Size 16in
  Brakes. . . . . Honda

Other

Fender.. . . . . Handmade
Rear fender .. . . Part of the steel body, handmade
Fuel tank.. . . . . Stretched Coffin
Dashboard. . . . . Handmade & integrated into the body
Handlebars . . . . Pullback Buckhorn
Headlight . . . . Square Bates (2)
Taillight.. . . . . Devil's Eye
Saddle .. . . Handmade
Homemade/
special parts . . . . Body, frame
Colour .. . . Pearl White with gold leaf inlaid by Prudon Paint

it – and it was suddenly right in front of his nose again. John could do nothing but buy it.

It was 1976 when Honda launched the Gold Wing 1000 to compete with other big bikes being produced in Japan. The first Wings were naked bikes, which only later appeared as touring models. The wide engine block was not really suited for a slim chopper build, but the huge power and torque, and especially the quiet motor, was an ideal project for relaxing cruising in Europe. Hence, Moto Lux in Holland saw a challenge to not only build a Honda custom bike for itself, but also to develop a whole line of accessories at the same time. Back then a relatively small company, Moto Lux, became one of the largest international suppliers of custom parts and accessories for Japanese engines known under the name Highway Hawk.

Custom builders were a thinly sown breed in the '70s, so when John started working for Moto Lux about 25 years ago, it was his job to establish a custom dealer network in Europe. Moto Lux was one of the first companies involved in importing and converting Honda, Harley, and Yamaha bikes, and other engines now regarded as classics. With the digital age still in the distant future, few images of chopped engines from America were available as templates for chopper projects. It was a time that heralded the beginning of the custom bike era. There were very few motorcyclists compared to now, and an even smaller percentage of rebellious custom bikers. These guys met and formed clubs, many of which still exist today. The conversion of bikes had begun, and increasingly choppers came to life in the Netherlands.

During these early years, Dirk van Wijk and Geert Prudon were custom builders who had done much work for Moto Lux; hence Geert had been commissioned in 1976 to build the Gold Wing Chopper. The engine and gearbox were the only parts that remained original: the rest was custom-made. And back then this was not so simple; the technique, parts, tools, everything was really quite different! This meant that it really all had to be handmade. Typical for these years (remember that we [Dutch custom scene] really lagged far behind on American style) were, of course, the Girder front fork, square exhausts, the long, deep low rider-style frame, and above all, the Velvet and the wild, almost Baroque-style, paint job (with real gold).

Later on, John and his wife, Karin, started a business in Gold Wings and associated accessories. John's hobby is to restore old Wings to their original state; hence he's always been on the lookout for older Wings. How did the chopper come into his hands?

John: "I love crazy motorcycles. It was not surprising, when I saw a photo on the internet about 12 years ago of a white GL 1000 chopper, that I directly responded to it. I knew this chopper already from my Moto Lux period.

"I really wanted the bike in my shop for customers to enjoy. The seller turned out to be a great collector, and before long I was the new owner of this classic white beast. I also bought the red trike featuring next from the same owner."

Gold Wing trike

TECHNICAL DATA

Owner . . . . .Biker's Best	Gearbox	Fork . . . . .Springer
Builder . . . . .Dirk van Wijk (DPP)	Year. 1976	Wheels, brakes & tyres
Brand. . . . . .Honda	Type . . . . .GL 1000	Tyres . . . . .Dunlop Whitewall
Model . . . . .Gold Wing GL 1000 Trike	Link.. . . . . .Act clutch	Front wheel . . . . .Springer front wheel 21in
Engine block	Final transmission .. . . .Shaft drive Suzuki Jeep	Brakes. . . . . .Small, chrome Springer style
Year. 1976	Frame	Rear wheel. . . . . .Suzuki car wheel rim
Displacement. 1000cc	Year. 1977	Size 235/70-85
Ignition.. . . . . .Dyna	Builder . . . . .Dirk van Wijk (DPP)	Brakes. . . . . .Suzuki
Exhaust system .. .. . .Short Drags	Shock absorbers.. . . .Suzuki	

LARRY HOUGHTON, UK

Larry's 'Wide Boy' Honda CBX-based custom came third in the Freestyle class at the 2010 London Ace Cafe Motorcycle & Custom Show. The six-into-six exhaust system took Expressive Engineering three weeks to build, requiring seven meters of stainless steel tubing.

SPECIFICATION

- Custom-made frame using one-inch thick aluminium sheet
- Front end similar to BMW Telelever system
- Single-sided Ducati 916 swingarm at the rear
- 17in Marchesini wheels from a Ducati 996
- Gunmetal Black paint job overlaid with dusted silver and finished with orange pinstriping

This custom is based on a 1983 six-cylinder CBX.
(Courtesy Floris Velthuis)

Six-into-six exhaust system.

What a fine custom it turned out to be!

Next follows a window onto more Honda trikes ...

CYCLE EXCHANGE, US

Cycle X is a shop in the north woods of Wisconsin that produces everything required to build great Honda cycles and trikes.

SPECIFICATION – CB750 TRIKE (FRAME & REAR END)

- Boxer-style front section or Pro Street front section
- 7in longer than stock rear length
- Honda or HD neck cups for multiple front end options
- Positive traction
- Limited slip differential
- Disc brake callipers (both sides)
- 51-tooth 530 chain
- Heavy-duty bearings
- 40in width
- Gm 5-4.75 bolt pattern
- Optional oil tank & battery tray
- And, of course, Cycle X style

Below: The Honda Shadow trike turned-out rather well. Seen at the Great American Motorcycle Show at the North Atlanta Trade Center, Atlanta, GA. (Courtesy Mark Hamilton)

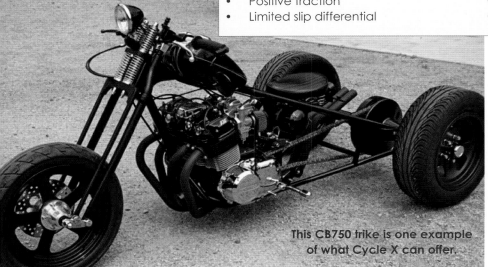

This CB750 trike is one example of what Cycle X can offer.

THE TRIKE SHOP, UK

The Trike Shop is a small, friendly, family owned business that has been producing big results for some time. The company is proud to have won numerous awards for its innovative style and engineering. Several of its trikes featured in magazines, film and television productions, and have attracted a host of celebrity customers.

The team, fronted by Haydn and his wife Bev, have over 50 years' experience in the motorcycle industry.

The shop also specialises in adaptations for the disabled rider, is a NABD Gold affiliated business, and is proud to have had a long affiliation with the National Association for Bikers with a Disability (NABD). More Trike Shop trikes will feature later in this book, too.

The Honda DN-01 trike

Trike Shop: "This trike was specifically created with the disabled in mind. The motorcycle itself is a 700cc shaft drive automatic, so lends itself well to a wheelchair user.

"We fitted twin-lever braking, so the rider can operate both the front and rear brake from the handlebar. If you look closely at the rider footrests, you will see there are plates with metal guides on. This helps tremendously for those without control of their legs, providing a secure rest for the feet; the guides preventing the foot from slipping or vibrating off.

"A rider backrest was also fitted for support, partly for comfort and partly to offer a more secure ride. At the rear of the trike you can see a very large rack. This was designed to carry a wheelchair. The rack unlocks and rotates so that the rider can load their wheelchair, swinging the rack back to its resting position and

locking in place via catch locks. Most wheelchair users have chairs that allow them to quickly and efficiently remove the wheels for this very purpose. We fit separate wheel locks on the racks, so it is all safe and secure.

"This Trike was sold to the NABD (National Association for Bikers with a Disability), to promote the fact that disability should never hold anyone back. It really is worth looking at its website (www.nabd.org.uk)."

DN1 trike in standard trim.
(Courtesy onEdition)

This was likely the first Honda DN1 trike conversion.

TECHNICAL DATA	
Type	Liquid-cooled four-stroke 8-valve SOHC 52° V-twin
Displacement	680cm³
Bore x stroke	81 x 66mm
Compression ratio	10:1
Max power output . . .	45kW / 7500min-1 (95/1/EC)
Max torque	64Nm / 6000min-1 (95/1/EC)
Carburation	PGM-FI electronic fuel-injection
Throttle bore	40mm
Air cleaner	Viscous, cartridge-type mesh net filter
Fuel tank capacity . . .	15.1L (including 3L LCD-indicated reserve)
Ignition system	Fully transistorised electronic
Clutch	HFT with internal hydraulic control
Clutch operation	Automatic
Transmission	HFT (Human Friendly Transmission)/ Continuously variable transmission
Final drive	Enclosed shaft

Honda NXR1800 (Purple) 'The Rune'

Trike Shop: "When we originally purchased this bike for conversion we paid extra for the chrome upgrade ... which turned out to be only a chrome front wheel! We decided the chrome had to be accented, so made sure the rear wheels were chrome too.

"This Trike belongs to one of our Scottish customers. It's a coincidence that the only two Runes we've created are in Scotland."

SPECIFICATIONS

- Trike Shop UK LTD conversion
- Triple chrome wheels (rear 245/30ZR20)
- Kliktronic
- Reverse gear
- Reverse link front end
- Stainless trike arms
- Rider footplates with rails & velcro straps
- Twin shock rear end
- Twin-brake lever mounted on handlebars

Front suspension via trailing bottom link with 3.9in travel.

A very well-executed custom.

Elevated rear view.

VALKYRIE CUSTOM TRIKE

The Valkyrie model lends itself to trike conversions. This custom Valkyrie trike was spotted in England. (Courtesy Adrian Pingstone)

HONDA GOLD WING TRIKE

A Hannigan-built custom Gold Wing trike from the US. (Courtesy Freddie Maupin Sr)

TECHNICAL DATA

Engine	1832cc liquid-cooled horizontally opposed six-cylinder
Bore x stroke	74 x 71mm
Compression ratio	9.8:1
Valve train	SOHC; two valves per cylinder
Fuel delivery	PGM-FI with automatic choke
Ignition	Computer-controlled digital with three-dimensional mapping
Transmission	Five-speed
Final drive	Shaft
Front brakes	Dual full-floating 330mm discs with three-piston calliper
Front tyre	150/60R-18 radial
Wheelbase	68.9in
Seat height	27.2in
Dry weight	794.0lb
Fuel capacity	6.1 gallons

Honda Pan European 1100 V4

The Honda Pan European 1100 V4 engine makes a fine basis for trike projects.

This trike was built by Sooty Reynolds in the UK.

John Ziemba Restorations, UK

The JZR pictured here is a replica kit of a British sporting three-wheeler by Morgan, manufactured in the UK by John Ziemba Restorations. The kit comprises a steel construction for the integrated, square tube chassis with galvanized lower body sheet metal. The upper body is composed of fibreglass. This kit is often used with Honda CX500-650 or ST1100 V4 engines, as well as Moto Guzzi 850-1000 or Harley Evo-powered variations.

A Honda ST1100-engined JZR kit car photographed at Whaley Bridge, Peak District, Derbyshire. (Courtesy Martin Alford)

This chapter concludes with two examples of Honda street quads ...

Stanley Benham, US

Stan: "The idea for a street-able quad in my head goes way back. In 1994, while on my VFR, I skidded on some oil when stopping for a car blocking the highway. As I was sliding and rolling, it occurred to me that I really needed something for the road that had four wheels ...

"In 2001 Cannondale released an all-aluminium quad. It dawned on me that I could weld the front frame rails onto a street bike, so I'd have a four-wheeled machine that is still classed as a street bike.

"I began searching for a suitable bike. Knowing the level of complexity involved, and how much drag the bike would have, I decided on a high-power motorcycle. The CBR1100XX was a good match, and the most available at the time.

"I acquired a bike that had been wrecked after only 1000 miles and a Cannondale frame, and began considering how best to bring it all together. I finally concluded, after many sleepless nights, that the best thing to do was simply to start cutting and live with the results. After two days I had fitted and welded it together. Another two days and I had modified the swingarm. With the bike assembled, I tested it to find that the engine was oil starved in the corners and that the bearings spun. After solving the oiling problems, I went to the safest place I knew to test something like this: the Sandhills.

"Two years on, I still hadn't broken it, and decided it was time to make it street legal. As of 2011, I'd ridden the bike 25,000 miles in 20 states, and trailered it just as far to numerous locations with my wife, to ride every type of road I could find. This amounted to as many as 650 miles in a single day, and as many as 4000 miles per trip.

CBR1100XX quad in the field.

At the top of Pike's Peak.

"The fastest I have ridden it is 135mph at Bonneville, and winding trails, like those leading to Pikes Peak, make for as much fun as you can have on a bike, although I prefer tarmac roads. I have ridden with the Blackbird Owners Organization on many occasions, and spirited rides are the best."

HONDA GOLD WING QUAD

Hannigan Motorsports in the US used a two-wheel front end, replacing the standard Gold Wing's single front wheel of its usual trike conversion, to create this luxury quad.

The Hannigan HRT Roadster Gold Wing GL1800 quad. (Courtesy Will Femia)

CHAPTER 2
KAWASAKI

Kawasaki started its custom LTD motorcycle range in 1976, and by 1980 all Japanese bike manufacturers had custom versions of their standard singles, twins, or fours on the market. By 1982 cruisers made up over 40 per cent of all bike sales in the US.

The two bikes at the top of this page are early '80s Kawasaki cruisers.

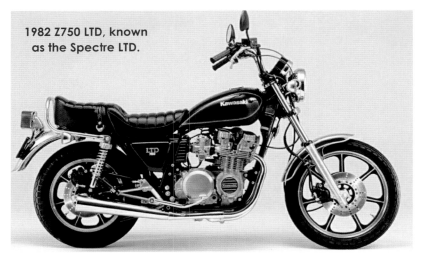

1982 Z750 LTD, known as the Spectre LTD.

Kawasaki Z440 LTD twin from 1981.

Below: Kawasaki promotional brochure featuring the Eliminator. The ZL900 was produced for two years only, and was the only bike in its segment at the time to have an inline four rather than V4 power plant. (Courtesy Kawasaki)

KAWASAKI ELIMINATOR

The Kawasaki Eliminator was introduced in 1985, as a drag style bike with a bobbed rear fender, short travel fork, large rear tyre, big chromed mufflers, a small fuel tank and low straight bars. This power cruiser's engine was derived from the liquid-cooled, inline four-cylinder, Kawasaki Ninja ZX900 unit.

The ZL range with the inline four engine was later available in 400, 600, 750 and 1000cc guise. The Eliminator name was also used for small capacity singles and twins under EL125, EL175, EL250 and VN250 designations.

ELIMINATOR

Of course, there's more to riding than tearing up a quarter mile of asphalt.

Anyone can twist a throttle, but not everyone handles a curve as well as a stoplight. Not everyone demands good handling, brakes, tires—and knows how to use them.

We built the Eliminator for riders who want it all.

Nothing is fake. The revolutionary profile is amazingly clean. Low, lean, and overflowing with muscle—it looks like it rolled out of a master customizer's garage.

Check out the wide, flat, roomy seat. Slide forward, slide back—there's room enough for two. If you want comfort, nothing matches this.

Let your hands fall to the bars. Masterful and straight-forward. No white knuckles in town, no aching arms on the highway.

And you can't miss the massive rear tire. More than six inches wide, it's the biggest, stickiest rear rubber ever mounted on a production bike.

Just one more reason why you and your Eliminator will be catching more eyes than anything else in town.

2000 VN250
Eliminator.
(Courtesy
Kawasaki)

KAWASAKI VULCAN

1984 saw the start of Kawasaki's Vulcan cruiser range, using mostly V-twin power plants, ranging from 125 to 2053cc (125in^3). The Vulcan 500 series, produced 1990 to 2009, was the exception in that it was powered by a 498cc parallel-twin rather than V-twin engine.

The Vulcan 750, produced 1984 to 2006, was the company's first V-twin. The bike was also available as 699cc in the US until 1986, due to tariff restrictions.

The engine derived from the Kawasaki Ninja 500R model, also known as the EX500 or GPZ500S. (Courtesy Kawasaki)

The modern, cruiser style VN800A came to light in 1995, featuring a softail design, 21in front wheel, and bobbed rear fender. A 16in wheel Classic version followed suit in 1996.

2004 VN800 Classic: liquid-cooled, 4 valves per cylinder, V-twin. (Courtesy Kawasaki)

The 800cc Drifter, built between 2000 and 2006, with its deeply valanced fender skirts evokes memories of the Indian Chief V-twin. The Drifter design was developed from a custom motorcycle built by Cobra USA in May 1996, and found its way into production initially as a 1500cc version.

Rear air shock absorbers and progressive front suspension made the Drifter a comfortable cruiser.

The Vulcan 800 Drifter from above.

A later 903cc (55.1in³) Classic edition in action. (Courtesy Kawasaki)

2010 Vulcan 900 custom featuring a 21in cast front wheel and 180mm rear tyre. (Courtesy Kawasaki)

2008 VN1600 model. (Courtesy Kawasaki)

Vulcan Mean Streak VN1600. (Courtesy Kawasaki)

2009 VN1700E (104in³). (Courtesy Kawasaki)

The Vulcan 900 range superseded the 800 series from 2006 onwards.

The Vulcan 1500 series (Classic, Mean Streak and Drifter) was built 1991-2008. The 1600 series was produced between 2002 and 2009 in Classic, Nomad and Mean Streak guise.

Since 2009, the Vulcan 1700 series has ruled the roost. The bike pictured left has a 52-degree SOHC, liquid-cooled, fuel-injected V-twin equipped with six-speed transmission and ride-by-wire throttle.

From 2004 onwards Kawasaki also produced the biggest Japanese V-twin to date, the Vulcan 2000 series.

Below, left: This 2005 2053cc (125.3in³) 52° V-twin sure has presence. (Courtesy Kawasaki)

Kawasaki custom bikes can come in all shapes and sizes, depending on what is available or desired by their builders ...

DARIZT DESIGN, INDONESIA

This custom bike is based on a 1981 Kawasaki KZ200.

Agus: "I almost completely modified the original frame to extend the wheelbase. The front suspension is from Yamaha Byson, and the rear is from Daytona. I sourced the tank from an old junkyard motorcycle (my best guess is a Zundapp) and modified it. Some parts were taken from a bicycle, such as cable and cable holders.

"The cylinder head was bored up. The piston was replaced by a larger one from an '80s Honda Civic. The carburettor was changed to a 32mm Mikuni item. Lastly, I upgraded the ignition and wiring."

Exhaust pipe, handlebar, saddle and rear fender are all handmade. The forward controls and footrests are made from a bicycle crank and bottom bracket.

ALFRANCH CHOPPERS, BUENOS AIRES

This Kawasaki-powered custom was built
by Alfranch Choppers, Buenos Aires.
(Courtesy Cuto Producciones)

Amazing what
you can do with
a Kawa Z440 LTD.
(Courtesy Cuto
Producciones)

LOUIS STANDS, US

This custom began as a stock 1998 Vulcan Classic 800cc.

Louis: "I had seen some other builds using the stock tank, which just didn't work for me. To do this bike properly, it needed a classic Sportster tank, and a bit of work to the backbone and deleting the stock thermostat made room for this.

"The seat was made by a leather worker who specializes in horse saddles; it was just what the bike needed to get that trim, skinny look.

"This was my first bike build and just as much fun to build as to ride."

The stock pipes have been customised, and apparently sound great.

The bike is lowered 2in front and rear, so it sits just right.

The rear fender is a slightly shortened Blue Collar Bobbers item.

METAL MALARKEY ENGINEERING, UK

The Kawasaki W650 is another model that's becoming more and more ripe for customising.

CLAUS THEILE, US

In 1976, Claus bought a new Kawasaki 750 twin in Germany. He shipped the bike to the US when he emigrated in 1987, to build a custom from it.

Claus: "I welded and manufactured the hardtail and a lot of the smaller parts, such as brake and gearshift levers, electrical box and sissy bar. The fuel tank is from a '70s small Yamaha. The fork and rear rim are from Sweden. The rear tyre is a 155/15 VW tyre with tube which easily lasts 40,000 miles. The rear chain runs in a grease-filled case, so each chain lasts about 40,000 miles. The bike had over 110,000 miles on it when I finally stopped counting. The 750 twin produces 50hp. Fuel consumption is 50mpg."

A lovely W650 bobber by Metal Malarkey Engineering.

Mufflers are straight pipes with VW inserts.

The factory crankshaft counter balance system was removed to enjoy true twin engine vibration.

Kawasaki custom by Donald Branscom. The frame is a DNA rigid; 6 up, 4 out, with 42° rake, and modified. The wheel setup is 240mm rear wheel and 21in front.

DONALD BRANSCOM, US

Donald: "The engine for this build was sourced from a 2004 Kawasaki 1500 V-twin. It came from the factory with twin plug heads, hydraulic lifters and liquid cooling. This model had one carburettor.

"I tried the radiator behind the engine and it worked, but it put a lot of heat around the rider. If the radiator was farther aft it would work ok too. I designed the direct chain drive, eliminating nine parts and 60lb of weight! These shaft drive motorcycles are therefore overweight, and Kawasaki switched to belt drive on later models."

HOTSHOECUSTOMS, US
Kawasaki Chopper Fortune Cookie KZ

Shannon 'Shoe' Gower from Hotshoecustoms was approached by customer Sean to build a special bike. Where so many motorcycles powered with vintage metric engines come to fruition because of money constraints, this one came into being because Sean wanted to ride something radically different from the standard fare found rolling down the road.

Shoe: "When such opportunities present themselves, I offer up something from my 'vault-o-vintage-goodies;' in this case a '73 vintage Kawasaki Z1 dragster carrying a hotrod '77 mill that I had been hoarding for a decade. Although about half of my work – truly

some of my best – is based around the venerable Harley Davidson drivetrain, I love, and ride, metric motorcycles."

A pattern had to be made first to get the arched backbone and the dropped height in the steering head. Gooseneck frames are usually at an angle, sloping toward the ground. This was the 'Fortune Cookie' inspiration; a near 90° downtube to a radius backbone to get the look. Amongst many other aspects, keeping the lines of the bike clean required making custom brake lines and running them through the frame and handlebars, joining the front and rear brakes to a central proportioning valve. With it, the other controllers and standard variety of electrical components were squeezed into the box sitting on the lower frame rails.

Shoe: "Having completed the bike, watching this scoot roll down the street, freed from my imagination, I couldn't have been prouder: how neutral the steering was and how light it felt; how it leaned against the grain when parked to clear space in a roadside line-up; how it got brought to life with a trick modern pass card and flew with a bullet that is three decades old; how it turned into a truly unique custom motorcycle with not another one like it on the road."

Fortune Cookie, with its very low seat height, vintage-style whitewall tyres and springer front suspension.
(Courtesy Shoe & Bob Feather)

A Kawasaki trike rounds off this chapter ...

Part of the design brief for Fortune Cookie was getting the neck dropped from the maximum chassis height of an arched backbone. The bike also features a credit card ignition system, and a jockey shifter.
The bike is fitted with DNA parts, such as a springer fork in a custom shortened length, handlebar controls, risers, drive sprocket/four-piston brake and matching front brake setup.

This trike is powered by a Kawasaki Z100ST, and was owned by J Eadie in Scotland. (Courtesy Alan Kempster)

CHAPTER 3
SUZUKI

Suzuki's early custom models began as lightly converted road bikes. Motorcycles like the GS550/750L fours, or GS/GSX 250-400 twins in the late '70s to early '80s, featured peanut tanks, stepped seats, smaller rear wheels, and such like.

The first Suzuki custom cruiser was the LS650 Savage single, released in the mid '80s, followed by the Intruder V-twin line of cruisers ranging from 400 to 1500cc.

The Intruder 1400 was produced from 1987 to 2005, and it proved that Suzuki could produce a big, clean cruiser with a strong chopper influence. The long-running model achieved cult bike status in Germany, due to its reliability and ideal basis for customising.

The 1400cc engine displaces 83in³, and has a four-stroke air/oil-cooled V-twin with single overhead cam. The six-valve engine has a bore and stroke of 3.70 x 3.85in and compression ratio of 9.3:1. The Intruder features an electric starter and five-speed transmission with a shaft drive.

In 2005, Suzuki revamped its cruiser lineup by consolidating its Intruder, Volusia, Marauder and Savage designations under the Boulevard banner.

The Intruder in its Suzuki S83 Boulevard incarnation, produced until 2008. (Courtesy Suzuki)

2005 Intruder/Boulevard 250LC. (Courtesy Suzuki)

Boulevard S50 had a water-cooled 45° V-twin. (Courtesy Suzuki)

2011 Boulevard S40 featured a 652cc (94x94mm) air-cooled SOHC engine. The S designation stands for the company's standard cruisers. (Courtesy Suzuki)

2010 Boulevard C50, formerly the Volusia 800. (Courtesy Suzuki)

2009 M90/ VZ1500 in full flight.

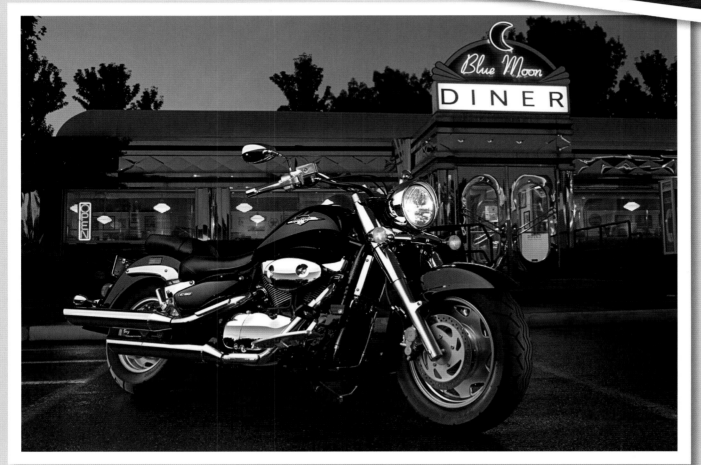

2009 Boulevard C90 1500cc in posing mode. (Courtesy Suzuki)

The flagship classic Boulevard C109R/C1800R 2010. (Courtesy Suzuki)

The C designated Boulevard lineup represents the more classically-styled cruisers.

The Boulevard M designation is reserved for the high-performance cruiser models in Suzuki's stable.

In 2007 Suzuki's US design centre penned the Suzuki Biplane concept. The bike was revealed at the 2007 Tokyo Motor Show. The aim was to offer the rider the sensation of flying in a vintage biplane without a canopy.

2010 Boulevard M50/M800, also based on the Volusia (Courtesy Suzuki)

Below & below, right: In 2011 Suzuki introduced this limited edition M109R Boulevard with custom paint. The close-up shows the rider's view of the instrumentation. (Courtesy Suzuki)

The semi-exposed V-Four engine concept. The cylinder heads and exhaust headers are visible each side. The front end has a girder-type fork and Buell-style rim-mounted brake discs. (Courtesy Evan Hayden)

Link-type rear suspension showing under the tractor-style seat. The exhaust is hidden underneath the cowling. (Courtesy Evan Hayden)

RNO CYCLES, NETHERLANDS

Arno Overweel is the man behind Rno Cycles. Always interested in all things mechanical, he developed the two-wheel bug in 1989. He's never looked back since, modifying every bike he's seen or owned to date.

With a background as a mechanical designer/manufacturer, Arno has an eye for detail, visual imagination, design skills, and extensive experience with various manufacturing processes and materials, which enables him to produce unconventional, out-of-the-box bikes.

Arno: "Using experience and innovation, I aim to create a practical and creative balance between form and function that is as unique as the riders themselves. Naturally, besides the character and design of the bike, reliability and safety are also very important to me."

Lucky Bastard

Arno: "I wanted to build an extreme, minimalistic bike. I noticed the Suzuki LS650 because of the large capacity of its single-cylinder engine. And once the bike is stripped of a lot of parts, it already looks quite nice: a good base to start from.

"During the build I decided I would enter the finished bike in a bike show. To cut a long story short, I had a fantastic time at the Bigtwin Bike Show in November 2007 where I won first prize in the Custom Class!"

TECHNICAL DATA

Engine	Suzuki LS650 Savage, 1 cylinder 652cc, 5-speed
Builder	Completely overhauled by Rno Cycles, painted & polished
Carburettor	Mikuni, with K&N filter
Exhaust	Stainless steel by Rno Cycles
Frame	Suzuki LS650, modified by Rno Cycles
Swingarm	Stainless Steel by Rno Cycles
Front fork	Suzuki LS650 overhauled by Rno Cycles Yokes by Rno Cycles (6° raked)
Front calliper	Nissin (Honda CBR900RR)
Rear calliper	Brembo
Hoses	Goodridge stainless steel
Various	Seat, handlebar, footpegs, battery box, sidemount by Rno Cycles
Extras	Countless custom, stainless steel handcrafted parts.
Awards	1st prize Bigtwin Bikeshow (Netherlands) 1st prize Open European Custombike Championship (Belgium)

This fusion bike has a handshifter with a clutch lever attached. Half of the Rno Cycles stainless steel tank is for fuel; the other half houses electrics. (Courtesy Floris Velthuis)

The exhaust is well integrated with the long and low appearance of this bike. The front wheel is a Honda CBR900RR 16in with a Bridgestone Battlax BT014 130/70 tyre. The rear wheel is a Honda CBR900RR 17in with Bridgestone Battlax BT014 180/55 tyre. (Courtesy Floris Velthuis)

Slick Chick

Arno: "Years ago, there was the idea of fabricating a mechanically driven turbo on my CB750. I would use the fresh snail house of an exhaust turbo from a truck and let it spin using the crankshaft. This idea 'ended up in the fridge' until it was time for a new Show bike.

"During construction of the 'Lucky Bastard' [outlined previously] all kinds of ideas arose for another radical single-cylinder bike. It had to be low and stretched. But what to do with the gap that arises between the engine and the rear wheel? You guessed it, the fridge opened, and there was an Eaton M45 supercharger.

"The name? 'Chick.' The motivation for the build, 'Slick.' If it doesn't blow, it sucks ..."

TECHNICAL DATA

Engine..	Suzuki LS650 Savage, 1-cyl 652cc, 5-speed. Supercharged by Rno Cycles (Eaton M45)
Carburettor	Dellorto 40mm with K&N filter
Exhaust	Stainless steel by Rno Cycles. Muffler by Laser
Frame	Rno Cycles Hardtail 2010
Front fork.	Suzuki LS650, 70mm shortened, overhauled and modified by Rno Cycles
Front wheel	Suzuki LS650, rim powder coated, hub polished, stainless steel spokes. Dunlop Roadsmart 110/80 19 tyre
Rear wheel	Aprilia RSV Factory, powder coated, Dunlop RoadSmart 190/50 17 tyre
Front brake	Calliper: Tokico. Front disc: MotoMaster outer ring, Rno Cycles inner ring. Hose: Motoacc
Bodywork	Tank by Rno Cycles, headlight by MCS, Mohawk by Rno Cycles
Various	Battery box/tank, seat, controls & sidemount by Rno Cycles
Handlebar.	Protaper. Magura front controls
Awards.	Best of Show, Rogues MC Choppershow

Slick Chick strikes a lovely pose. The bike features an Rno Cycles hardtail frame and Eaton M45 supercharger. Arno is a fan of small [read, very small] fuel tanks. Not to compromise, a fuel pump is used on this custom to pump the fuel from the large tank to the small one. (Courtesy Floris Velthuis)

METAL MALARKEY, UK

Malcolm Shepherdson started Metal Malarkey Engineering more than ten years ago. He has a toolmaker/welder background, and he worked as foreman with MRD Métisse building classic racing chassis.

His company specialises in motorcycle frame manufacture, specialist welding, and in advanced design and development projects.

This custom has been finished to a high standard, with quality parts used throughout.

SPECIFICATION

Customer	Bart Reid
Motorcycle	Custom built
Colour	Black
Component parts supplied by customer	
Engine	Suzuki GSXR1100. Bandit sump
Complete front end	GSXR 1100
Rear wheel	GSXR 1100
Footrests	GSXR 1100
Speedo	Digital speedos – Koso
Seat	Dragon
Oilcooler	HEL
Brake reservoirs	Jap 4 Performance
Component parts supplied by Metal Malarkey	
Petrol tank	Zodiac; Roundside Sportster-style
Petrol tap	Zodiac; Pingel
Rear mudguard	Zodiac; 9in rigid type
Electrical components	Zodiac; latch relays
Indicators	Ball end
Oil, brake & clutch lines, rear brake light switch	HEL
Headlamp	Custom Fasteners. Bates 5¾in Halogen
Stainless fasteners	Custom Fasteners
Rear light	Alien
Indicators	Ball end
Air filters	Conical
Chain	Mike Pearce; 530 o'ring
Throttle & cables	Triumph speed triple

Services	
Wiring	Phil James
Paintwork	Joe Prichard – Candy Customs
Engine paint	Nigel – Graham's Garage
Powder paint	Cambrian Powder Coaters, Oswestry
Design	Metal Malarkey / Bart Reid
Frame	CDS2
Top tube	1.75in x 12swg.
Other tubes	1.25in x 14swg.
Rake	30 degrees
Ground clearance	6in
Other	Rigid design. Tig welded.
Parts fabricated by Metal Malarkey	
Frame	
Stainless exhaust system (tucked in – ground clearance)	
Stainless seat base pivot	
Electrical box (housing battery, coils, starter solenoid, relays & fuses)	
Rear mudguard struts	
Rear light brackets	
Assembly	
Metal Malarkey. Stainless Fasteners used throughout	
Road testing	
Metal Malarkey, Bart Reid	
Comments (comfort, road-holding, satisfaction/grinfactor)	
Surprisingly comfortable	
Very 'sure-footed'	
Causes great interest everywhere	

ROADHOUSE MOTORRÄDER, GERMANY

Roadhouse Motorcycles has been in existence since 1997, and modifies everything from Harleys to metric bikes. The single-cylinder engine of the hardtail custom bike shown below was sourced from a Suzuki DR800.

Bullseye indicators are very much in fashion in Germany.

SOOTY'S CUSTOMS, UK

Ian Reynolds' shop is concerned with custom, chop, street fighter, low rider and monster bikes.

Sooty's Suzuki hardtail gixer.

JOHN HOPKINS, UK

John: "I can't take credit for most of the build, I just completed an unfinished project really. The engine was ported, and I had to increase

Long and low, with some go.

Close-up of the engine/carburettors.

the jet size as it was running a bit rich. This should have increased the power by about 5-6hp. The paint was okay, but the tank was not so good, so a friend resprayed it in MG Teal Blue, which was as near to the original paint as possible. I added an oil pressure gauge and a different speedo, as well as a new battery. It's not a tourer, though a comfortable ride thanks to the mono shock, but the bike is so low you have to pick your routes, avoiding speed bumps!"

THUNDERBIKE, GERMANY

This German company began operating in 2006 as a Harley Davidson dealership. It is also an acclaimed customiser of Harley and Suzuki/ Yamaha metric bikes, something company founder and bike builder Andreas Bergerforth recently proved again by winning the 9th annual AMD World Championship of Custom Bike Building 2012 at the Sturgis Motorcycle Rally with his PainTTless Harley custom entry. Below are three examples of the firms many Suzuki custom options.

Above: Suzuki VL1500 Result. A very well-executed metric custom by Thunderbike.

Left: Bagger/touring conversion of a Suzuki VL1500, the Fleetwood by Thunderbike.

FLEETWOOD: CUSTOM PARTS USED
Windshield by King Size, lower deflector by Leggings, license bracket by Fleetwood, 4.5in chrome headlight by Bate Style, Beachbar chrome handlebar, Riser polished, Riser adapter set, grip set V-Tech polished, custom stretch tank by First One, 4-piston Spiegler calliper, 4.5in Passing light bracket, Fleetwood fender modification, front and rear whitewall tyres, Fleetwood hardbag, master cylinder cover.

Nice flowing lines.

FIRST ONE: CUSTOM PARTS USED
Frame cover set, polished choke cover, polished ignition switch cover, Monocok solo seat, Ram-Air oil cooler, polished Cat-Eye license bracket, polished dual headlight bracket, Candy 4.5in chrome headlight, Riser adapter set, custom lever set, polished forward control kit, Gisela front fender, Classic chin fairing, First One custom stretch tank, 4-piston calliper Spiegler chrome, Triple tree Racing Performance polished, Beefy polished fork cover set, swingarm modification open, custom tank, Spiegler Race 230 brake kit, custom brake disc.

Suzuki VL1500 First One.

THE YORKSHIRE CHOPPER, UK

The images of this Suzuki-powered custom bike in Yorkshire are courtesy of Brit Chopper, UK, and what a stunner it is!

TECHNICAL DATA

Builders	Ian Thompson & Mark Graham, North Yorkshire, initially built as a softail painted in black
Owner	Mick Collings, who changed it to a hardtail, with more ground clearance, twin seat & new paint
Engine	Suzuki VS1400
Frame	By Mark & Ian, using 2in CDS seamless, hand bent, tig welded
Exhaust	Short stainless pipes
Rear wheel	Custom-made, 280 tyre
Rear brake	Honda Fireblade calliper, stainless brake lines
Forks	Standard, polished, yokes handmade from highgrade alloy
Handlebars	Mark Graham
Fuel tank	Extensively modified Harley Sportster tank
Electricals	Under fuel tank
Engine cooling	Earl's oil cooler
Rear mudgard	Modified Harley item
Paint job	Powder coated frame. Tank & rear guard wet painted then lacquered (Wizard Paint, Malton)

Above: The front wheel is hand-built on a stainless rim, with a 200/70 tyre. Below: Out on the prowl!

The bike looks long, low and purposeful.

The standard carburettors are bolted on to two handmade manifolds.

LMC – Lang Motorcycles, Germany

Hans-Jürgen Lang's company began in 1998. It has since become one of the country's pioneers in the Dragstyle and New Style chopper custom scenes. LMC's focus is on customising Japanese cruisers, especially the Suzuki VS1400 Intruder.

Since LMC's inception, three frame variations were developed, namely the Basicline, Tribleline and Hardline concepts. Since 2000, the company has won 25 prizes in European custom shows.

LMC: "We are focusing firstly on the look and the line of our bikes. But the rideability is at least as important to us as the look! We sometimes heard comments from onlookers like 'this is just a show bike.' But from our experience we can claim that the converted Intruder with a well-tuned chassis rides better than the original.

"We also offer four different stages of motor tuning, if customers require more power from the VS1400. Stage one starts with 1450cc (85hp and 98Nm), and stage four goes to 1700cc (110hp and 165Nm).

"Lastly, we also work on converting Harley's, Yamaha's or Kawasaki's into custom bikes."

Black Witch

TECHNICAL DATA	
Model	Hardstyle
Built	Frame 2001
Engine	VL1500 original
Output	84hp
Carburettor	Original with power kit
Air filter	K&N
Ignition	Original
Exhaust	Miller Evo 1 adjustable
Transmission	Original
Gears	5
Secondary drive	Shaft drive
Paint	Kreis Design
Frame	Original VS1400, heavily modified with Hardstyle-frame alteration
Swingarm	S&S wide swingarm kit 10.5in
Suspension rear	Bitubo with LMC cover
Foot rest equipment	TB/V-Tech
Rim, front	NLC 4.5x17in
Front tyre	150er
Rim, rear	NLC 10.5x18in
Rear tyre	280er
Front brake	LMC left side, Wave brake disc, RST 4-piston brake saddle
Rear brake	LMC Hardline
Fork bridge	LMC Hardstyle
Fork cover	LMC Hardstyle
Front fender	LMC Bandit
Rear fender	LMC Hardstyle
Seat	LMC Hardstyle
Battery cover	LMC Hardstyle
Tank	LMC special
Headlight	LMC Hardstyle
Handlebar	LMC Hardstyle
Hydraulic instruments	Rebuffini
Switches	Rebuffini
Brake & clutch cables	Goodridge
Miscellaneous	LMC front spoiler, LMC number plate holder, LMC cylinder cover, LMC oil cooler integrated with the frame, LCD-speedo integrated with the fork setup

The rider sits *in* rather than *on* the Black Witch.

The LMC oil cooler is integrated with the frame.

Oldstyle

The Intruder Oldstyle, just begging to be ridden – a lovely piece of work. (Courtesy Sabine Welte)

TECHNICAL DATA – OLDSTYLE

Model	Oldstyle
Built	2007
Engine	VS1400 Intruder
Output	67hp
Rear fender	Oldstyle
Air filter	K&N
Ignition	Original
Exhaust system	Custom-made
Transmission	Original
Gears	5
Clutch	Strengthened
Secondary drive	Shaft drive
Paint	Studio Luftpinsel
Frame	Oldstyle frame conversion
Swingarm	Original
Suspension, rear	Bitubo
Foot rest equipment	RST
Rim, front	Original rear wheel with cover-drum brake look
Tyre, front	170/80-15
Rim, rear	Original
Tyre, rear	200/80-15
Front brake	RST 4-piston Springer
Rear brake	RST 4-piston
Fork	Springer fork
Seat	Oldstyle/convertible to swing saddle
Battery cover	Stainless steel coated
Tank	Original
Headlight	Oldstyle
Riser	4in Springer
Hydraulic instruments	Custom
Switches	Custom
Brake & clutch cables	Goodridge
Miscellaneous	Sparto rear light, carburettor kit, grips, Oldstyle fuel tank lock, real gold coating!

The VS1400 also lends itself to triking ...

VS1400 custom trike pictured at the 2006 Royal Bath and West show ground, UK. (Courtesy Peter Wort)

THE TRIKE SHOP, UK

Trike Shop: "This performance trike was created for a disabled rider. We fitted Kliktronic, which allows the rider to change gear by pushing buttons on the handlebar, rather than via a gear pedal. We also fitted twin lever braking, so both front and rear brake controls are on the handlebar, because the rider was not able to use a conventional brake pedal setup.

"The rest of the motorcycle was left standard (including the paintwork) – other than completing a trike conversion. We do not modify the actual frame of the motorcycle; our usual fixing points for a trike axle are where the shock and swingarm are mounted.

TECHNICAL DATA – SUZUKI GSX1300R HYABUSA	
Conversion.	Trike Shop UK Ltd
Top speed.	190mph
¼-mile acceleration. . . .	10.4 sec
Power	175bhp
Torque	99ftlb
Weight	215kg
Seat height	805mm
Fuel capacity	22 litres
Average fuel consumption	35mpg
Tank range.	160 miles
Insurance group.	15
Engine size	1299cc
Engine specification . . .	16v, inline 4, 6 gears
Frame	twin spar
Front suspension adjustment.	Preload, rebound, compression
Front brakes	Twin 320mm discs
Front tyre size	120/70x17in

"A completely standard Suzuki GSX1300R Hayabusa was used. This particular motorcycle is a chain drive high-performance sport bike that Suzuki released in 1999. It immediately won acclaim as the world's fastest production bike, with a top speed of 188 -194mph (303-312 km/h)."

Lastly, a rare picture of a custom-painted Hayabusa street quad ...

The sports handlebars were replaced so that the rider could sit more upright.

Hayabusa street quad at the Carlisle Motorcycle Fest in Carlisle, Pennsylvania in July 2010. (Courtesy Phoebe Pitassi)

CHAPTER 4
YAMAHA

XV750 62hp V-twin, with a 75° angle between the cylinders, mono shock rear suspension and shaft drive. (Courtesy Yamaha)

The dual shock XV1000, produced from 1988. Offset cylinders helped cooling air to reach the rear cylinder, eliminating any need for liquid cooling. (Courtesy Yamaha)

Yamaha was another manufacturer to enter the cruiser sector, initially with lightly modified road bikes from 1978, with models such as the XS400 SE and XS650SE twins, and its XS750 SE triple.

The Virago XV750SP released in 1981 was the first Japanese V-twin cruiser, and a serious attempt by Yamaha to claim some of the big V-twin market from Harley Davidson.

The Virago was redesigned in 1984. The mono shock was replaced by dual shock absorbers, and a teardrop fuel tank was fitted. From '84 to '87 engine capacity was reduced from 750cc to 699cc to counteract the US tariff imposed on motorcycles over 700cc.

The Virago series was produced from 1981 to 1999 in the following engine displacements: 125; 400; 500; 535; 699 (700); 750; 1000; 1100cc.

1988 XV535. Successor to the XV500SE introduced in 1984. The XV535 received a face-lift in 1989 in the form of a bigger fuel tank. (Courtesy Yamaha)

The Midnight Special XV1000SE, produced from 1982. (Courtesy Yamaha)

In 1994 Yamaha launched the new standalone brand name Star Motorcycles for its cruiser range in America. Outside of America the same cruisers were sold as Yamaha bikes.

The Star Motorcycles range is designed in the US. The Drag Star, XVS and V-Star range of cruisers covered the following engine displacements: 125; 250; 400; 650; 950; 1100; 1300cc. Further Star models were produced under the Royal Star, Stratoliner, Roadliner/XV1900 and Road Star XV1600 designations.

The Virago 535 was replaced by the XVS650 Drag Star in 1997, followed in 1999 by the release of the XVS1100 Drag Star sibling.

Yamaha's 2014 Star Bolt R performance bobber is a rather attractive offering.

The 650 Drag Star became a worthy successor to the XV535.

1100 Drag Star, with its 65in³, SOHC, air-cooled, 75° V-twin, is a powerful bike.

A double-down-tube steel frame gives the 2012 Yamaha V-Star 950 the longest wheelbase in its class.

TECHNICAL DATA – BOLT

Model	XVS95CEB/C; XVS95CEW/C
Engine	58cu³ (942cc) air-cooled four-stroke, V-twin, SOHC, 4-valve
Bore x stroke	85.0 x 83.0mm
Compression ratio	9.0:1
Fuel delivery	Fuel-injected
Ignition	TCI (Transistor Controlled Ignition)
Transmission	5-speed multi plate wet clutch
Final drive	Belt
Suspension, front	Telescopic fork, 4.7in travel
Suspension, rear	Dual shocks, 2.8in travel
Brakes	Wave type discs, 298mm
Front tyre	100/90-19M/C 57H tube type
Rear tyre	150/80-16M/C 71H tube type
L x W x H	90.2 x 37.2 x 44.1in
Seat height	27.2in
Wheelbase	61.8in
Ground clearance	5.1in
Fuel capacity	3.2 gal
Est Fuel economy	50.9mpg
Wet weight	540lb
Colour	Raven; Pearl White

This bike will certainly take a slice out of Harley's Sportster market.

The 2012 Yamaha V-Star 1300 is powered by a 1304cc, fuel-injected, liquid-cooled, V-twin engine.

The 250cc class offers an affordable entry point to motorcycling, and should not be underestimated in its importance for the survival of the breed. Many 250cc V-twin bikes, like the Virago 250cc, have been stepping stones to Harley or bigger metric V-twin cruiser ownership.

The Star Raider represents a new generation of custom cruisers. The 1854cc (113in^3), fuel-injected, V-twin-powered Raider is loaded with custom parts, combining chopper-inspired styling with a superior handling chassis.

Yamaha's V-Max power cruiser was produced between 1985 and 2007. English designer John Reed was commissioned by Yamaha to design this muscle bike, based on the Ventura V4 engine. Its 1197cc (73in^3), liquid-cooled, DOHC, 70° V4 engine was noted for its quick acceleration, and gained quite a following over the years.

2012 Yamaha V-Star 250. Its heavyweight styling and lightweight packaging is ideal for novice riders.

The 2012 Star Raider is customised right out of the crate, with a stretched out fork, fat rear tyre, low seat, and a slammed riding position.

The 2012 Star Raider SCL is a very limited edition Custom Raider S. Its high-metallic Blazing Orange paint, coupled with a metal flake and shine made possible by a six-layer paint, was specifically created for this bike. Its custom 5-spoke chrome wheels were co-developed by Star and Performance Machine, with matching chrome pulley and chrome belt guard.

A Star custom on display at the 2008 Cycle World Motorcycle Show in Atlanta. (Courtesy Mark Hamilton)

2012 Star Stryker, featuring a 1304cc, fuel-injected, liquid-cooled V-twin engine and classic belt drive.

78

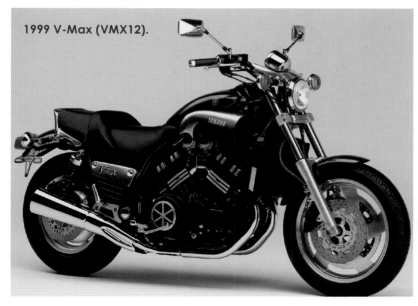

1999 V-Max (VMX12).

2012 Yamaha VMAX (VMX17), featuring a 1679cc (102in³) engine and significant power and performance.

In June 2008 Yamaha officially released a completely redesigned successor to the original V-Max brute for 2009, called the VMAX.

MARK'S BIKE WORLD, TAIPEI TAIWAN

Established in 2005, this bike shop buys and sells motorcycle parts and accessories while specialising in customising motorcycles. Mark Huang always had an interest in modifying his own rides, while pursuing a degree in International Trade at Chinese Culture University.

Once he finished his degree he partnered up with his younger brother to create their own garage to indulge in their hobby of building bikes. The two of them have been building bikes and riding out their passion ever since.

Mark: "The Crazy Arc build was one of the more drastic chops I've completed to this day. The chopper scene in Taiwan is still fledgling due to intolerable government regulations towards customising motorcycles, so we have very limited resources for building our bikes and the process can often take a long time when compared to the likes of US or Europe. This meant that the entire build, from inception to completion, took the best part of a year.

The oil tank is positioned between the rear wheel and the engine on Crazy Arc.

TECHNICAL DATA	
Model	The Crazy Arc
Builder	Mark Huang, Taiwan
Owner	Gregory Wu, Taiwan
Engine	SR400
Exhaust	Custom
Transmission	Stock
Forks	Custom
Chassis	Custom
Length of bike	220cm
Suspension	Custom
Fuel tank	Custom
Fenders	Custom
Seat	Custom
Front wheel	Firestone 3.00-21in
Rear wheel	Firestone 5.10-18in

"Except for the stock engine, everything was either handmade or purchased from other vendors (ie wheels and lighting). The owner had very few restrictions on budget and simply wanted something that had never before been seen in Taiwan. So I decided to go all out with this build and give it a unique oil tank with an opening through the middle, banana girder forks, and a custom seat that looks more uncomfortable than it actually rides. Lastly, the paint was done by Jeffrey Chang of Air Runner Custom Paint. It's a local paint studio that is garnering more and more international recognition."

Crazy Arc custom.

JvB-Moto & KEDO, GERMANY

Jens vom Brauck and KEDO built this custom (right), dubbed the SR 500 D-Track. The bike is a mutant cross between a '60s desert racer and Kenny Robert's '70s flat track bike.

Thanks to Kedo, the Hamburg-based SR and XT tuning and parts specialist, the bike featured a hotted-up SR motor (up to 50hp) equipped with a Mikuni round-slide carburettor, Harley Sportster style fuel tank and serious-looking swingarm. Jens vom Brauck did the rest.

Jens: "We've forgotten what biking is about. It's all about feeling: the sound and the rhythm of the motor, the contact with the machine. It should be unfiltered, direct. We've got too sophisticated. The D-track goes back to the roots. It has a lot of soul, and in the real world, away from racetracks and autobahns, it's fast, and its performance is accessible – very nice indeed."

The black rims, machined alloy swinger, Wilbers shocks, high-level exhaust and big carburettor with an open filter give the bike a raw, competition look without being intimidating.

At 170kg there isn't much obvious 'fat' on the SR500, but Jens' 'diet' junked 25kg of assorted old iron and plastic bits, replacing them with only a few kilos of stainless steel, alloy and sculpted composite materials created by the designer.

The Japanese Bonneville – aka Yamaha's venerable XS650 – is a very popular platform for customising, and three examples follow ...

LC FABRICATIONS, US

The LC Fabrications XS650 was initially in the company's workshop as a friend's unfinished project. During some downtime, Jeremy Cupp decided to give it a new lease of life. The result is a tracker-style custom with a hardtail rear end.

Jeremy: "In trying to keep it similar to our other bikes, we hardtailed the stock frame, kept the stock front end, and moved the front wheel to the rear. The offset brake disc and small rear sprocket combination meant we could run both on the same side, so the front wheel was modified to accept this setup and moved to its new location at the rear of the bike. To keep both brakes on the left side of the bike, we used an XS1100 dual disc front wheel and left-side calliper, then shaved the unneeded parts from it, including the right leg. The stock front end was bolted up using tapered bearings and custom trees, which were designed to work with the front shroud we cut from a piece of aluminium sheet. The bars

The fuel tank is a modified Honda Scrambler item.

The frame is a stock Yamaha/LC
Fabrications hardtail. The rake is stock,
and the stretch in the tail section is 3in.

TECHNICAL DATA

Owner .. .. Jeremy Cupp
Shop .. .. LC Fabrications
Yr/make/model.. .. .. .. 1979 Yamaha XS 650
Fabrication .. .. LC Fabrications
Build time .. .. 4 months

Engine

Size.. .. .. 750cc
Builder .. .. LC Fabrications
Cases. .. .. Yamaha
Cylinders .. .. XS Performance
Head.. .. .. Yamaha
Carbs. .. .. Mikuni 36mm roundslide
Air cleaners .. .. LC Fabrications
Exhaust. .. .. LC Fabrications
Ignition.. .. .. Boyer/Brandsen

Transmission

Type .. .. Stock unit 5-speed/XS Performance
                                              overdrive
Clutch .. .. Barnett

Suspension

Front .. .. Stock
Rear .. .. None

Wheels, tyres & brakes

Front
  Wheel. .. .. 19in cast mag
  Tyre .. .. Bridgestone
  Disc.. .. .. Stock, drilled & moved to left side
  Calliper.. .. .. XS 1100 left calliper
Rear
  Wheel. .. .. 19in cast mag
  Tyre .. .. Bridgestone
  Disc.. .. .. Stock, drilled & moved to left side
  Calliper.. .. .. Brembo

Paint

Colour .. .. H-D blue/white
Painter .. .. LC Fabrications
Graphics .. .. LC Fabrications

Accessories

Bars .. .. LC Fabrications
Hand controls.. .. .. GSXR 750
Foot controls. .. .. LC Fabrications
Pegs .. .. LC Fabrications
Headlight .. .. LC Fabrications
Taillight.. .. .. LC Fabrications
Number plate mount.. .. LC Fabrications
Seat .. .. LC Fabrications

were then stubbed right into the thick aluminium upper tree, saving the need for clamps or risers of any kind.

"The tank was sourced from an old CL360 Honda that I had re-tunnelled and cut a 3in wedge out of the centre. The seat section was created from a small piece of flat rear fender that I wedged to match the tank, then I built the rest from 14 gauge sheet. The LED tail lights were made to fit in the rear.

"The original plan for the engine was to just split the cases, clean, inspect, and reseal everything. Once I got inside I was quite impressed by just how well-engineered this engine is. I hate to let a good opportunity go to waste, so I dug into some cash and ordered a beautifully re-cast 750 cylinder kit from XS Performance. For carburation I swapped the stock Keihin for 36mm Mikuni round slides. I continued with some mild porting, replaced all the gaskets, seals, timing chain and guides, then dressed up each piece as I reassembled my newfound engineering masterpiece.

"The paint colour was chosen by our local paint store. The colour was a mismatch left over from another job, but worked well with the black wheels. All the other details were created as I thought of them during the build, some of which went on to feature in our new line of XS parts. In the end I decided to name the bike Chicken Salad; a good explanation of what I thought I was starting out with versus what I was able to transform it into."

LIMPE IVEN, NETHERLANDS

Limpe began by sourcing all the essential parts for his XS650 custom, such as frame, motor, hubs and some small items.

Limpe: "I mocked up the parts, put the engine in place, and shortened the fork legs, which are from a XS750 Yamaha (1mm thicker and a simple fork stop without thread).

"Determined to get a good line for the hardtail section, I made a simple jig, then bent, welded and connected some tubes with slugs in the existing frame, before cleaning the welds and making them smooth.

"I wanted something that came from my own mind, combined with the images I'd seen in magazines over the years. It definitely helped that I had a degree in motorcycle mechanics, working on modern Japanese cycles every day, besides being a freelance photographer for motorcycle magazines.

"The engine was overhauled and the cylinders bored. I reworked the head myself, and fabricated stainless steel exhausts to my liking, running them inside the frame, without mufflers. Basically, every part is new, including a new set of Mikuni vm34 because the stock carburettors looked too large.

"The bike is running on points ignition, and the charging system has been converted to run without a battery, although I fitted a small one for easy starting via kickstart (the electric starter has been removed).

"Other new parts fitted were new wheel bearings, steering head bearings, sprockets and levers.

"After assembly of the fabricated parts, I ran it for a couple of days to make sure the frame (especially the hardtail section) was up to the task. On bare metal you can easily see cracks, after the paint job it's a lot harder. The handling was fine, everything ran smooth and nothing seemed to be a problem, so I disassembled the bike ready for painting. The green metal flake paint was applied by a friend who owns a car paint shop.

"After paint and assembly, the bike went to another friend to be pinstriped. I gave him complete freedom to use his expertise to create what he thought looked best. I love the resulting gold leafed upwards flame design, which definitely adds to the look.

"I never really rode it enough, so sold the bike to someone who made me a great offer."

Desired features were ape hangers, long pipes, and a hand shifter with the hardtail frame.

The front wheel is constructed around a 21in, 36-spoke rim and 1971 hub with Yamaha XS650 twin-leading-shoe drum brake, and Avon Speedmaster tyre. The rear hub and rim are stock items.

METAL MALARKEY ENGINEERING, UK

Yamaha XV535 customs are rare. This hardtail version was pictured at Sabah Bike Week, Malaysia. (Courtesy Harn Sheng)

BOYZCHOPPERS, US

Bare Bones XS650, built in the Japanese Bratstyle fashion.

The team put an '80s XV1000 engine in this hardtail-framed chopper.

MICHIEL DE MOLENAAR, NETHERLANDS

Michiel is a Dutch geology student with a passion for building motorbikes. The first bike he converted was a BMW café racer, built on the sidewalk outside his parents-in-law's place.

This '80s XV920 Virago-based custom was built with a friend of his.

TECHNICAL DATA

Handlebars	Homemade, from modified, reversed Solex brake and clutch handles
Headlight	Fog light from a tractor
Frame	Raked, the front made longer
Steel fairing	Homemade
Rear fender	Made from a front fender
Tail light	Homemade
Seat	From an antique bicycle, mounted on a section of leave spring from an MGB sports car
Inlet manifold	Homemade
Exhaust	Homemade
Fuel pump	From a rally car
Speedometer	Suzuki SP370
Number plate holder	Made out of a pulley-puller (tool)
Battery box	Homemade, stainless steel
Wiring loom	Homemade
Forward controls	Homemade
Brake pump	BMW R75

The bodywork is homemade. The Solex downdraft carburettor stems from an Opel Kadett B car.

THUNDERBIKE, GERMANY
Yamaha XVS1100 'Custom'

This XVS1100 custom has a Competition chrome 2-2 flat exhaust system and Sunbeam 8.5x18 rear wheel with Metzeler ME880 240/40/18.

Sunbeam 4.5x18 front wheel on Metzeler ME880 130/16/18 with swingarm conversion 3D8.5x18.

SPECIFICATION
- Front spoiler
- Hyper charger
- Recall front fender
- Sunbeam brake discs
- Dual headlights
- Lowered forks
- 16-litre fuel tank

The Yamaha XV1600 was a popular platform for customising. Here are three examples ...

The XV1600 'Black Out'

'Black Out' features a Tricky Ride air suspension kit and Freestyle swingarm kit.

SPECIFICATION

- Powerfilter smooth Competition VA Big 2-2 exhaust
- V-Tech footrest setup
- Time Crack handlebar
- Snake headlight
- Freestyle smooth pulley cover
- Recall front fender
- VA front spoiler
- Hardrace leather seat
- Freestyle 4.50x18 front wheel
- Metzeler ME880 60V tyres
- Freestyle brake disc

'Black Out' is fitted with a Freestyle 10.0x18 rear wheel on a Metzeler ME880.

SPECIFICATION

- Solo seat XV1600
- Cat Eye license bracket
- Beachbar chrome handlebar
- Dexter front fender
- Big Evolution rear fender
- 60er Dragpipes
- Spoke rear wheel
- Turn signal adapter
- Stainless steel lines
- Painting & airbrush

The XV1600 'Black Jack'

'Black Jack' has a modified swingarm and a lowering kit on original shock absorbers.

Xv1600 Ironside

The bike has
a drag-style
appearance.

SPECIFICATION
- Belt narrowed
- Offset 300 pulley kit
- Hard Attack steel
  rear fender
- Recall steel front
  fender
- Hard Attack seat
- Front and rear discs
- 4.5x18in front wheel
- Metzeler 880F
- V-Tech fuel pump
  cover
- Phantom grips-cross
- Freestyle smooth
  pulley cover
- 16-litre fuel tank
- Stadel blue
  headlight
- V-Tech fork bridge
- V-Tech footrest setup
- Competition VA Big
  2-2 exhaust
- Hypercharger
- Tricky Air Ride
  suspension kit

11.0x18 rear wheel
on Metzeler ME880.
Rear disc brake
and a Starfire 300
swingarm set.

LAZARETH AUTO-MOTO, FRANCE

Ludovic Lazareth has a background as an automotive designer and prototypist. His creativity and passion for muscle machines is well-known, resulting in innovative two-, three- and four-wheeled creations.

Ludovic formed Lazareth Auto-Moto in 1998 with the aim of offering a pleasurable and exclusive ownership experience of products from a modern, futuristic, forward-thinking, expressive and dynamic brand.

The VMAX Hyper Modified performance cruiser was born from a partnership with Yamaha Motor Europe, and is based on the new 1700 VMAX. The aesthetic was completely revised and updated to offer a cutting-edge, innovative style, inspired by the Manga universe. Cycle parts like the engine and frame come from the original bike, with an enlarged rear wheel, more powerful brake system and a lowered fork added. The VMAX Hyper Modified is available in Limited Edition and is street legal.

The VMAX Hyper Modified has a forward-lunging stance.

The aggressive, Manga-inspired look enhances the virility of the VMAX.

Lazareth Auto-Moto sells this bike on an ex-works (excluding transportation and taxes) basis. The customer receives a brand new 1700 VMAX customised as follows (original parts are sent with the bike upon request):

- Complete polyester body parts, R6 rear light with turn signal
- Handlebar with holding billet parts
- Custom seat
- Electronic instrument panel
- Upper headlight
- ISR master cylinders
- Durits kit for fluid brakes and clutch
- Polyester part for plate number and light
- Large rear wheel and 240 tyre
- Mufflers
- Special serial number plate and certificate of authenticity

AFT Customs, US

This custom from AFT follows the board tracker theme, and is called 'ER HED' (meaning Air Head).

ER HED was AMD World Championship metric class champion in 2008. The engine is from a 2004 Yamaha XVS Road Star, fitted with a Mikuni HSR 42 carburettor. The frame is a modified Redneck Engineering item, the exhaust is from AFT Customs, and the handlebars also function as the brake fluid reservoir.

TECHNICAL DATA – ER HEAD

Model	2004 Yamaha XVS17BT
VIN	JYAVP17Y64A000602
AFT Customs	Jim Giuffra/Ron Abel, Kylie/Elaina
Intake	Mikuni HSR42 Carb
Exhaust	AFT Customs
Paint	Scott Hultquist/ Riff Raff Customs, PPG 'Ruby Slippers'
Plating	Meclec/Black Nickle
Anodizing	LNL Idiots
Seat	Duane Ballard
Frame	Yamaha/Redneck Engineering, oil in frame custom design
Front suspension	RMD Billet Girder, Penske Shock
Rear suspension	Progressive suspension single shock
Wheels	RMD Billett 'Eiffel 23'
Tyres	Avon 130/60x23 Cobra
AFT Customs	Design, fabrication, handlebars, throttle, chain guard, rear fender, hydraulic clutch, cleavage cover, handlebar risers, exhaust, sparkplug, wires
All Balls Racing	Battery cables (custom)
Barnett	Clutch pressure plate
Baron Customs	Carb holder (custom)
Beringer Brakes	Radical pump master cylinder, Radical front calliper
Crime Scene Choppers	Air filter
CRG	Mirror
Chris Products	Tail lights
Dynatek	Coils, ignition module
Drag Specialties	Number plate
50's Boy Inc	Grips (custom)
HHI	Rear disc/calliper
Honda	Rear master cylinder
Independent Cycle	Headlight (AFT Customs modification)
Joker Machine	Rear master cylinder reservoir
Motion Pro	Throttle cable (custom)
Redneck Engineering	Frame, fuel tanks, gas cap
Vortex	Foot controls (custom) CIS sprocket
Works Connection	Master cylinder cap, dip stick
W8less Rotors	Front disc

JOHN REED'S GOLD YAMAHA, US

The Gold Yamaha is another 'blast from the past' custom bike. Way back in 1982, the bike took top honors at the Oakland Grand National Roadster Show in the US, and it reappeared at the 2011 World Championship of Custom Bike Building.

After his retirement from racing, John started Uncle Bunt's Chop Shop and gained considerable fame in his native England.

Yamaha wanted someone to promote its new V-twin cruiser in the early '80s, and Yamaha Europe approached John with a proposal to build a bike around its new engine, all expenses paid for.

The TR-1 V-twin 1000cc engine was all John needed, because he fabricated just about every other part of the machine by hand. His level of skill was enough for the Gold Yamaha custom to win the 1982 Oakland bike show, and in return international recognition of his work. As a result of this recognition, Custom Chrome Inc offered him a parts designer job in California, a role he held until his retirement.

Not known to be of the idle type, one of John's retirement projects was the restoration of the very same Gold Yamaha bike he'd originally created for the 1982 show. So, after 30 years, John vowed to show the restored bike once more, at the 2011 AMD event. The bike took 9th in the FreeStyle Class.

John Reed was inducted into the AMA Motorcycle Hall of Fame in 2001 for his contributions to motorcycling.

Photos courtesy of Onno Berserk Wieringa & AMDChampionship.com:

The detailing is amazing.

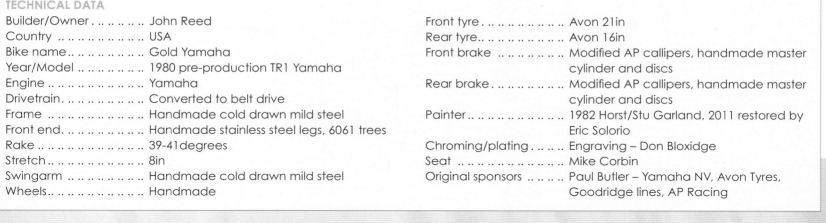

TECHNICAL DATA

Builder/Owner	John Reed
Country	USA
Bike name	Gold Yamaha
Year/Model	1980 pre-production TR1 Yamaha
Engine	Yamaha
Drivetrain	Converted to belt drive
Frame	Handmade cold drawn mild steel
Front end	Handmade stainless steel legs, 6061 trees
Rake	39-41degrees
Stretch	8in
Swingarm	Handmade cold drawn mild steel
Wheels	Handmade
Front tyre	Avon 21in
Rear tyre	Avon 16in
Front brake	Modified AP callipers, handmade master cylinder and discs
Rear brake	Modified AP callipers, handmade master cylinder and discs
Painter	1982 Horst/Stu Garland, 2011 restored by Eric Solorio
Chroming/plating	Engraving – Don Bloxidge
Seat	Mike Corbin
Original sponsors	Paul Butler – Yamaha NV, Avon Tyres, Goodridge lines, AP Racing

Everything except the tyres and rear belt was handmade or modified by John Reed in 1981 – art in metal.

A long and low stance.

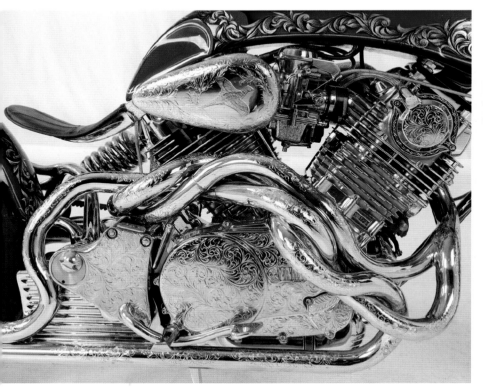

Exhaust close-up.

YAMAHA-BASED TRIKES FROM THE UK

Triking is very popular among the UK biking fraternity, and three good examples follow.

Virago custom trike.
(Courtesy Ernie Horler)

Another variation on the Virago trike theme.

Inline four Yamaha trike powered by a 1988 XJ900F engine.

TRIKE SHOP, UK
Yamaha MT-01 'Evil Twin'

Trike Shop: "We created the Evil Twin trike for someone who wanted to make a statement: right from the massively chunky 345/35-18 rear tyres, accented by chrome spinners on the rear wheels, to the overstated 300/35-18 front wheel!"

Much of the trike remains standard; the aggressive look is what the owner was so keen on.

SPECIFICATION – 4CYL YAMAHA XJ900F TRIKE

- Owner: Kevin Ashton
- Custom hardtail frame by Projex
- KTM Duke 2 forks
- Harley rear wheel fitted as the front wheel, 200 wide
- Billet yokes by Projex
- Custom stainless steel exhaust by Projex
- Custom handlebars, clock (dash panel), battery box, electric box and seats by Projex
- Ducati 748 exhaust silencers
- Front guard and mounts by Projex
- 8x15in rear wheels
- Harley Quick Bob petrol tank
- Billet foot rests and mounts by Projex
- Reliant Robin rear axle

TECHNICAL DATA

Displacement	1670.00cm³ (101.90in³)
Engine	V2, four-stroke
Power	88.90hp (64.9kW) @ 4750rpm
Torque	150.30Nm (15.3kgf-m or 110.9ft-lb) @3750rpm
Compression	8.4:1
Bore x stroke	97.0 x 113.0mm (3.8 x 4.4in)
Valves per cylinder	4
Fuel system	Electronic fuel-injection
Fuel control	OHV
Ignition	TCI
Lubrication system	Dry sump
Cooling system	Air
Gearbox	5-speed
Final drive	Chain
Clutch	Wet, multiple-disc
Driveline	Constant mesh, 5-speed
Frame	Alu CF-die cast, double cradle
Trail	103mm (4.1in)
Front suspension	Telescopic forks
Front suspension travel	120mm (4.7in)

Yamaha VMX1200

Trike Shop: "The VMX1200 was not altered in any way, and the trike axle we built for it was one of our standard conversions. Having created trikes for years, we feel this style of conversion is one of the best for motorcycle aficionados!

"It keeps all the looks of the motorcycle it was created from, and the end result looks like Yamaha could have made this itself! The only slight alteration from the norm is the way we upswept the exhaust, as always we look for clean lines."

TECHNICAL DATA

Displacement	1671.58cm³ (102.00in³)
Engine	V4, four-stroke
Engine details	Forged aluminium pistons and NGK® Iridium sparkplugs with R1-type direct ignition coils
Power	197.40hp (144.1kW) @ 9000rpm
Torque	166.80Nm (17.0kgf-m/123.0ft-lb) @ 6500rpm
Compression	11.3:1
Bore x stroke	90.0 x 66.0mm (3.5 x 2.6in)
Valves per cylinder	4
Fuel system	Fuel-injection with YCC-T and YCC-I
Fuel control	DOHC
Ignition	TCI (Transistor Controlled Ignition)
Lubrication system	Wet sump
Cooling system	Liquid
Gearbox	5-speed
Final drive	Shaft drive (Cardan)
Clutch	Slipper clutch
Fuel consumption	8.71L/100km (11.5km/L or 27.01mpg)

YAMAHA TESSERACT

This quad bike concept was first displayed at the 2007 Tokyo Motor Show. The quad is a hybrid vehicle, powered by both a V-twin engine and an electric motor. Yamaha equipped the concept with 'dual-scythe' suspension, which allows the vehicle to lean like a regular two-wheeled bike. When stationary the extra pair of wheels and a dual arm-lock system keep the Tesseract upright.

The Tesseract on display at the Tokyo Motor Show 2007. (Courtesy Evan Hayden)

This VMX1200 is a classic example of a trike conversion. Everything except the reverse gearbox is standard.

LAZARETH AUTO-MOTO, FRANCE

Ludovic's factory near the Swiss border produces unique car/bike hybrids, such as Wazuma. The R1-engined bespoke quad is one of the most advanced vehicles ever designed by Lazareth; a whole new concept based on an atypical 'W-wheeled geometry.'

To achieve a vehicle with maximum performance, matchless driving sensations and enhanced safety, Lazareth had to combine the best technologies from the automotive industry, and to think even beyond.

All Wazumas are numbered, manufactured to order, and fully customisable. 'It's not a car. It's not a bike. It's a Wazuma!'

TECHNICAL DATA

Engine	4 inline, 4-stroke, DOHC, 16v, crossplane crankshaft
Capacity	998cc
Bore x stroke	78.0 x 52.2mm (3.1 x 2.1mm)
Power	133.9kW (182ps) @ 12500rpm
Torque	Approx 115.5Nm (11.8Kg-m) @ 10000rpm
Frame	Lazareth design
Wheelbase	1500 ±35mm (59.1 ±1.38in)
Transmission	6-speed
Suspension	Adjustable
Tyres	
Front	195-40R17
Rear	245-40ZR17
Brakes	
Front	Double disc ø310mm (12.2in)
Rear	Single disc ø220mm (8.7in)
Dimensions (L x W x H)	2150mm x 1500mm x 1050mm
Dry weight	403kg
Top speed	250km/h (yet to be verified)
0-100Km/h	4.1 seconds
400m standing start	11.9 seconds

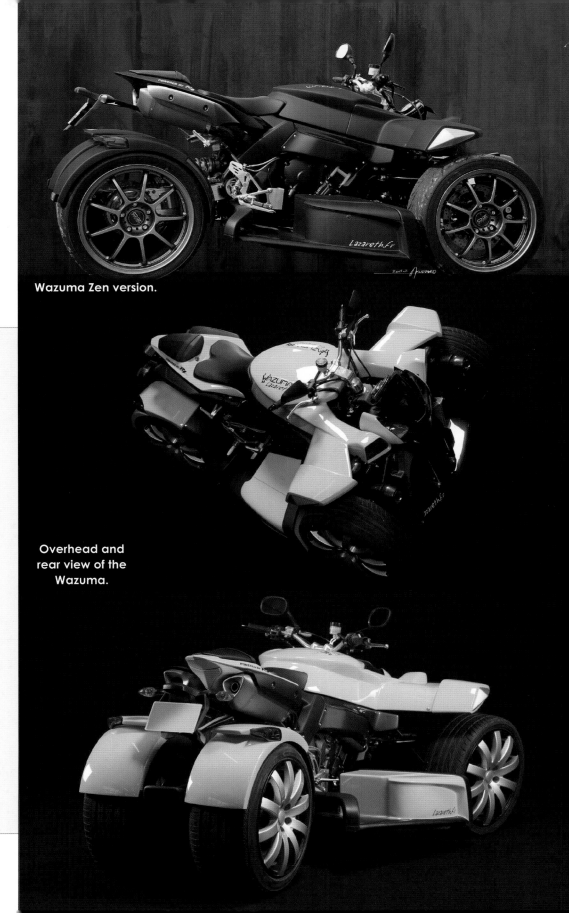

Wazuma Zen version.

Overhead and rear view of the Wazuma.

CHAPTER 5

JAPANESE DOMESTIC CUSTOM SCENE

Motorcycles are prevalent in Japan, so it comes as no surprise that there is also a very active domestic custom bike culture. The difference to the US or Europe is that, in the land of the rising sun, smaller bikes rule. Most are limited to between 250cc and 400cc due to licensing restrictions. This isn't to say that there aren't any bigger capacity machines on the road, it's just that anything over 400cc is costly to maintain.

The cult bike for customising in Japan has to be the venerable Yamaha SR400. The bike has been in production since 1978 and features an air-cooled, 4-stroke, overhead cam, 2-valve, single-cylinder engine, plus a good old kickstart to fire it into life. The SR400 has been the platform for countless café racers, street trackers, bobbers and choppers.

But the buck doesn't stop here. This chapter intends to present a wide range of Japanese custom bike creativity from a select number of local shops. For anyone intending to travel to Japan, there are four major custom bike shows where local builders display their wares:

- West Japan Motorcycle Show in Hiroshima, March
- Joints Custom Bike Show in Nagoya, April
- New Order Chopper Show in Kobe, July
- Hot Rod Custom Show in Yokohama, December

MOTO GARAGE LIFE

Hitoshi Kugizaki's custom shop is located in Wakayama, in the Kansai region of Japan. The outfit converts everything from Honda Cubs right through to Harleys. A selection of its work follows.

Kawasaki Vulcan 400 custom

TECHNICAL DATA	
Engine	Standard
Frame	Standard
Tank	Honda TL125
Light	6in Bates type
Tail lamp	Custom
Seat	Custom
Exhaust	Custom
Handlebars	Custom
Front fork	Standard, lowered
Rear suspension	Standard, lowered
Tyres	Firestone

Moto Garage Life custom based on a Kawasaki Vulcan 400.

Kawasaki Z250LTD custom 1

The chunky wheels dominate the bike's otherwise slim appearance.

TECHNICAL DATA

Engine	Standard
Frame	Standard, remodeled
Tank	Custom
Light	Bicycle light, remodeled
Tail lamp	Custom
Seat	Custom
Exhaust	Custom
Handle	Custom
Front fork	Standard, lowered
Rear suspension	10in
Tyres	Firestone

Left-hand view of the Kawasaki Z250LTD custom.

Kawasaki Z250LTD custom 2

TECHNICAL DATA

Engine	Standard	Exhaust	Custom
Frame	Custom	Handle	Custom
Tank	Wassell	Front fork	Normal low down
Light	4.5in Bates type		
Tail lamp	Custom	Rear suspension	10in
Seat	Custom	Tyres	Firestone

Another Kawasaki Z250LTD version.

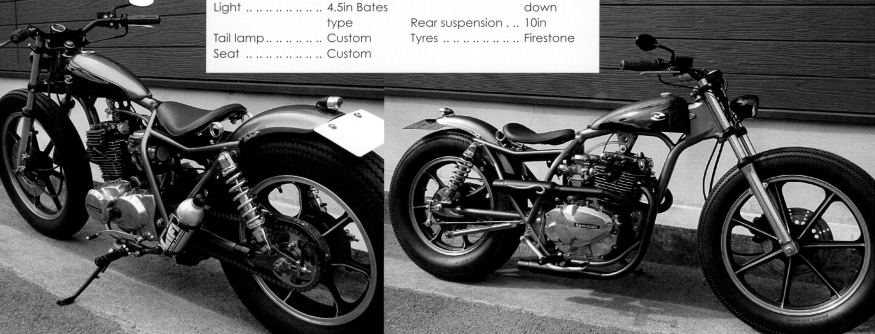

Heiwa Motorcycles'
Yamaha SR400 with
minimal fuel tank and
front and rear lights.

HEIWA
MOTORCYCLES

Kengo Kimura's custom
shop operates from
his home in Hiroshima
and was founded in
2005. Kengo prefers his
creations to be narrow
and low in appearance.

SR400 with narrow front
wheel.

Heiwa's XS650 taking over the road.

The W650, with its classic engine appearance, makes a willing custom platform.

Heiwa's classy XS650.

TOGURO'S (SHINSUKE TOKURA) LONG FORK CHOPPER

Toguro bought his 1992 Yamaha XV250 when at university in 1999. The now Japanese traditional wood sculptor has given his bike several do-it-yourself custom treatments since then. In 2003 Toguro hit his limits as a D-I-Y builder and commissioned Osaka-based custom shop Madmakers to realise his ideas further.

Toguro, pictured here hitting the highway, had Madmakers work on this bike for two years at a total cost of about 2,500,000 yen (2005).

TECHNICAL DATA

Front wheel	21in Invader for H-D (Arc system Pro Am, Japan)
Rear wheel............	16in Invader for H-D (Arc system Pro Am, Japan)
Digital master	Takegawa, Japan
Front fork	Handmade 32in over girder fork (Madmakers, Japan)
Fuel tank.............	Handmade prismic type (Madmakers, Japan)
Seat	Drug speciality, USA
Fender..............	Handmade fat bob (Madmakers, Japan)
Lights...............	Raybric back light for truck, Japan
Mirror, tail light........	Pro One, USA
Turn signals...........	Made in Taiwan
Front sprocket.........	13T for XV250, Japan
Rear sprocket.........	Handmade 45T, Afam
Carburettor	50cc racing type, Keihin, Japan
Air cleaner	Handmade diamond type (Madmakers, Japan)
Handlebar............	Handmade from same materials as frame
Balancing the front.....	Madmakers, Japan
Exhaust pipe	Handmade drug pipe (Madmakers, Japan)
Silencer.............	Handmade baffle (Madmakers, Japan)

MORE ONE-OFF CUSTOMS

This little bobbed custom started life as a Honda CB250, and is the work of Seigo Ikeuchi from Bodyline Specialties in Saitama. The moon covers over the spoked wheels look terrific. A rear drum brake provides stopping power. A nice contrasting shot of bike evolution, with the pink trike in the foreground.

This wicked Kawasaki Mach Chopper 'Flash Back' was crafted by Masao Ogawa from Kaikado Kustom Service in Komaki, Aichi District. (Courtesy Kazuyoshi Janta Ueda)

This bike is called TRINDA and it sports a Honda 450cc motor in a Triumph frame. The fuel tank is from a vintage Honda moped. Seen at a Mooneyes Custom Show. (Courtesy Motoyan)

A custom Honda Steed from privateer Hiroaki Nagatsuma. Classic ape hangers are not the only change to this bike.

KAVACH MOTORCYCLES

Beautifully captured at the 2010 Mooneyes motorcycle swap meet. This custom bike belongs to Ise Satoru, a chopper photographer famous in Japan. (Courtesy Shimobros)

Close-up of the fork and exhaust routing on this CB750 hardtail.

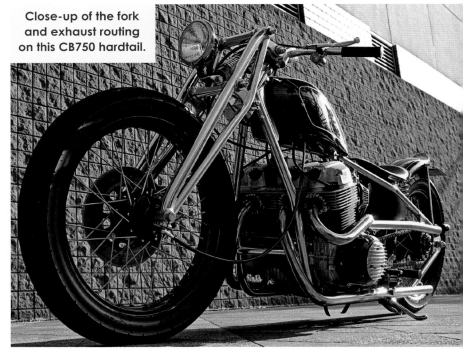

Kazu Yamaguchi's shop is located in Tokyo. His custom bikes are based on older Japanese engines, and some British sourced parts, such as frames and girder forks, are used. Kazu also produces various parts in his workshop. He points out that all his customs are certified vehicles in Japan.

Side view of this clean Kavach CB750 hardtail.

Kazu's Yamaha 750 Triple looks rather good.

Kawasaki
Kavach Z750FX.
It's a green,
mean machine.

MOTOR ROCK

Motor Rock started up in 2004 and is located in Nagoya. Keita Kobayashi and team have a big heart for customising SR400s, but it doesn't stop there ...

Kavach Honda CBX. A CBX hardtail is a rare sight.

This lovely custom is based on the Yamaha Drag Star 400.

Grass Tracker custom. The things you can do to a Suzuki single ...

I did say that Motor Rock creates custom SRs ...

TECHNICAL DATA

Basis	Stock SR400
Frame	Custom
Engine	534cc, with Mikuni/TMR carburettor
Exhaust	69 Megaphone Motor Rock
Fuel tank..	Motor Rock
Oil tank	Motor Rock
Rear fender	Motor Rock
Front fork cover	Motor Rock
69 Bar drag-style handlebar..	Motor Rock
Suspension	Easyrider, short
Seat	Custom, Razzle Dazzle
Wheels..	21in front, 15in rear
Tyres	Front Avon/SP MKII; rear Dunlop

This silver SR400 is an interesting bike to categorise ...

A Yamaha twin in new clothes. A TX750 engine is at the heart of this bike.

TECHNICAL DATA	
Donor bike	..Stock SR400
Frame	..Heavily modified
Engine	..Stock, Biller breather filter Motor Rock
Carburettor	..Keihin FCR
Exhaust	..Gravel Crew muffler, remolded
Handlebars	..69Bar Ltd style Motor Rock
Headlight	..Bates 5¾in
Taillight..	..Easy Riders, drilled

This SR400 custom runs on Excel wheels, with SP MKII Avon front tyre and Avon rear tyre. The fuel tank is a remolded Bonneville item.

Motor Rock's SR400 'Clock Work' with polished metal and chrome finish featured at the 20th Annual Yokohama Hot Rod Custom Show. The bike is fitted with a 74 Springer fork, custom handlebars, and a Dakota digital meter. The motor has a Keihin CR carburettor and K&N air filter.

Another Kawasaki custom, with raked front and Motor Rock pipes. The engine for this custom stems from a Vulcan 400.

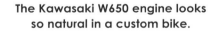

The Kawasaki W650 engine looks so natural in a custom bike.

TWO MORE GENRES OF JAPANESE BIKE CULTURE

The first example is an exotic replica of the *Akira* bike, based on a Manga serial from 1982 by Katsuhiro Otomo. *Akira* was made into an iconic anime feature film in 1988.

The bike was seven years in the making by enthusiast Masashi Teshima at a cost of $121,000.

It was taken across Japan to raise money for a children's autism charity. The bike's final destination was a Katsuhiro Otomo exhibit, also for charity; to raise money for victims of the 2011 earthquake/tsunami.

The second and last example is representative of the Bosozoku style of motorcycles, as used by a declining Japanese youth subculture. Bosozoku (translated 'violent running tribe') was/is known for riders embarking on massed rides, making lots of noise by removing the mufflers from their bikes, and engaging in reckless riding.

This is the only *Akira* bike officially approved by Manga creator Katsuhiro Otomo. (Courtesy Toshikazu Shibata)

Bright colours and high handlebars complete the Bosozoku package. (Courtesy Brunno Murasawa)

Oversized fairings and seat backrests are typical Bosozoku styling elements. (Courtesy Brunno Murasawa)

CHAPTER 6
CHINESE CLONES

This chapter presents some examples of Chinese-built cruisers or customs designed in the West, with hardware components sourced from China. Most engines used in these machines are based on older Honda or Yamaha designs. The enormous Chinese domestic market consists in the main of single- or twin-cylinder motorcycles and scooters, both rarely going beyond 250cc capacity.

Chinese two-wheeled vehicles chiefly compete with their Japanese counterparts in the West in terms of their affordability – just make sure that after-sales service and parts backup is assured.

Until recently, there has been an absence of bigger displacement Chinese bikes on Western markets, mainly because there isn't much call for them in the huge Chinese domestic market.

The annual CIMAMotor trade exhibition in Chongqing (in existence since 2002) claims to represent 90 per cent of Chinese production capacity. It is the largest expo for commuter motorcycles in the world, and where new product is introduced. Chinese products are here to stay, and it will be interesting to see what comes out of Chongqing in the future.

CLEVELAND CYCLEWERKS (CCW), US

CCW designs and assembles small displacement retro-type bobbers and café racers. The company's niche in the marketplace lies in providing inexpensive yet stylish motorcycles aimed at novice riders, of which 30 per cent are female.

CCW decided to source most components from China after it was turned away by US parts suppliers when setting up shop.

Scott Colosimo: "We have a cooperation with Lifan in China, from which we source our engines. Believe it or not, Lifan makes more motors a year than just about any other company. Quality is very high, hence we have many engines with over 100,000 miles.

"Our first motorcycle, 'tha Heist,' was launched in February 2010 at the Indianapolis Dealer Expo."

Cleveland CycleWerks is now manufacturing many components in the USA and in 2012 opened a new factory in Cleveland. Below are some customised Heist bobbers.

This hardtail bobber has a 12.5hp (9.3kW), 229cc (14in³), OHV single-cylinder motor. The engine design is derived from Honda's CG series.

'tha Heist' has a 24in (61cm) seat height and dry weight of 272lb (123kg).

BRIAN LILLY, US

Brian assembled the little custom pictured to the right from a Kikker Hardknock 5150 kit. He owns two Hardknocks: a 2007 110cc and a 2008 200cc model.

Kikker describes its design as follows:

"The Hardknock is a complete bobber kit in a traditional 'old-school' style, featuring forward controls, jockey shift, electric start, solo seat, hydraulic disk brakes, TIG welded rigid frame, vintage tyres, and optional springer front suspension. The kit can be ordered for either a 49cc, 125cc, 200cc or 250cc V-twin, 4-speed, four-stroke engine. There isn't any plastic on the Hardknock. It is comprised of numerous polished components and alloy steel, and can be ordered in black primer or in one of our custom paint schemes."

Brian: "The engines are Honda knock-offs. I call them 'Chondas' from China."

Brian's bobber has a Jockey shifter and sprung seat. The 200cc motor has been fitted.

Mission accomplished! Ed's Board Tracker, with 100cc Lifan engine.

ED WARGO'S BOARD TRACKER, US

Ed: "I am not a bike builder by trade, or an engineer. I have always enjoyed the look and nostalgia of the Board Track Racer, and wished I had enough money to afford a real one, but since that was going to be out of the question, I had to make my own.

"The build took me five years to complete, on and off. I am just a backyard, garage-type tinkerer, who had a vision for about five years prior to actually getting started. As time went on, I thought I had better get started or it will never get built!

"Believe it or not, I had never used a MIG welder before this, and actually borrowed one from a friend at work.

"There were no set plans, with the exception that it had to fit around the Chinese 100cc Lifan engine. The bike was completed in 2009, and basically has been sitting in the garage since. It was built for my enjoyment, and to see if I could actually do it."

MEYERBUILT METALWORKS, US

Cliff Meyer: "The bike started life as an idea my dad had. I had built a ¾-sized chopper for fun, and my dad took it for its first test ride around the neighbourhood. He was so hooked on it that he asked if I could build a full-sized bike. I told him I didn't see why not, and so began the Green Chopper project.

"My dad lives 3 hours from me. I did all of the work at my home, and he'd come to visit at weekends and help where he could. It was a lot of fun working on this bike together. Mainly I did all the fabrication and metalwork, and my dad supplied all his ideas and the money to get it done.

"The bike runs great and gets all kinds of attention. It won Best of Show at a local bike show. My dad rides it a lot, and he now wants to move up to a larger displacement engined bike. So, the next project is in the works."

SPECIFICATION
- 2007 Lifan 250cc engine – Yamaha clone
- Meyerbuilt Metalworks custom frame
- DNA 21in front wheel
- DNA 18in rear wheel
- Avon 2.15in front tyre
- Avon 200 rear tyre
- Meyerbuilt handlebars
- Meyerbuilt fuel tank
- Meyerbuilt fender
- Meyerbuilt stainless exhaust
- Meyerbuilt foot controls
- Meyerbuilt number plate holder
- Meyerbuilt wiring harness

This clean-looking bike sports a DNA Springer front end and Lifan engine. (Courtesy Casey Wilkinson)

LIFAN GROUP

The Lifan Group is a privately owned automobile and motorcycle manufacturer, founded in 1992. It is ranked as the third biggest motorcycle producer in China. Access to overseas markets was granted in 1998 and in no time Lifan become a global exporter.

JUAN GARCIA, VENEZUELA

Juan: "I own a Keeway 250 Cruiser, which I consider a good bike. It is a stable ride, with a top speed of 130km/h. Keeway is now one of the most marketed brands in Venezuela."

The Chinese company Qianjiang Group owns the Keeway brand, which produces motorcycles, scooters, safety equipment and ATVs. Launched in 1999 in the European Union, it now also has branches in South and North America, Africa and Asia.

TECHNICAL DATA

Model	Keeway Cruiser 250
Engine/transmission	
Displacement..	249cc (15.19in³)
Engine type	Twin, four-stroke
Power	18.10hp (13.2kW) @ 9450rpm
Torque	14.00Nm (1.4kgf-m or 10.3ft-lb) @ 7500rpm
Top speed..	115.0km/h (71.5mph)
Compression.	9.4:1
Bore x stroke	49.0 x 66.0mm (1.9 x 2.6in)
Fuel system.	Carburettor
Cooling system	Air
Gearbox..	5-speed
Starter	Electric
Fuel consumption	2.40L/100km (41.7km/L or 98.01mpg)
Brakes/wheels	
Front tyre dimensions.. ..	110/90-16
Rear tyre dimensions	130/90-16
Front brake	Single disc
Rear brake.	Single disc
Physical measures/capacities	
Dry weight..	150.0kg (330.7lb)
Power/weight ratio	0.1207hp/kg
Overall height..	1145mm (45.1in)
Overall length..	2300mm (90.6in)
Overall width	726mm (28.6in)
Ground clearance	150mm (5.9in)
Wheelbase	1530mm (60.2in)
Fuel capacity	14L (3.70 gallons)

This Keeway Cruiser custom looks like a mini Harley tourer/cruiser, and there's plenty of chrome to see.

CHAPTER 7
BOBBER BOLT-ON KITS

This final chapter is intended to provide further inspiration to the fertile brain of any potential customiser. The images to follow, taken by Randy Collier, show the work of Blue Collar Bobbers, a US company offering bobber conversion bolt-on kits.

Lance & Cheryl point out that their kits enable a conversion of one's standard cruiser into an old-school hot rod custom, and that just about any home mechanic can install them. The kits change the appearance of the rear fender (and the front fender on some bikes), lights, seats and optionally, the handlebars. Exhaust wraps and powder coating stock rims are further options to spice things up. The kits come with an instructional DVD to help installation.

Blue Collars is not into windshields, saddlebags or chrome. Its philosphy is pure bobber (ie to remove everything that is not needed), for the all important minimal look.

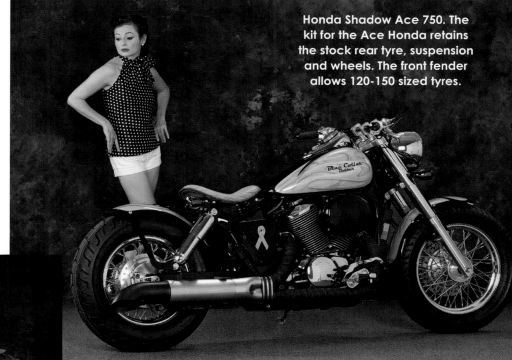

Honda Shadow Ace 750. The kit for the Ace Honda retains the stock rear tyre, suspension and wheels. The front fender allows 120-150 sized tyres.

Honda Spirit 750 Chain Drive (the Black Widow in some countries). A 2005 Honda Spirit provided the base for this army-styled bike. The stock handlebar risers were rotated 180 degrees, while using the factory drag bar. Blue Collar rear fender, license bracket, seat and lighting complete the package.

The Honda Rebel 250 kit fits bikes built from 1985 onwards. The factory fuel tank is retained, with no changes to the frame.

This bike started life as a 2007 Honda Spirit 750 shaft drive. Any Spirit models from 2007 onwards can have the seat, rear and front light, rear fender, vertical license kit or exhaust wrap changed, with the rear fender painted to match the stock bike. Installation time is claimed to be 14 hours. The bike retains its stock suspension and wheels.

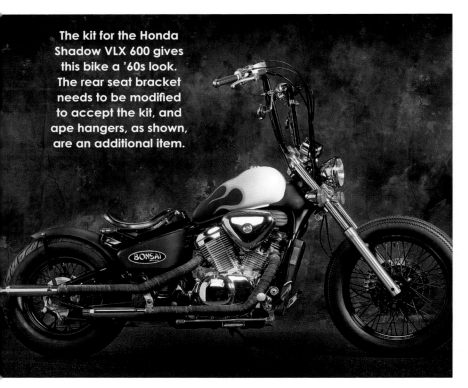

The kit for the Honda Shadow VLX 600 gives this bike a '60s look. The rear seat bracket needs to be modified to accept the kit, and ape hangers, as shown, are an additional item.

This Kawasaki Vulcan 900, with an Avon Speedmaster 5.00-16 fitted to the stock front rim, has a '50s flavour.

This long, low bobber is based on the Honda Shadow Aero (Phantom) 750.

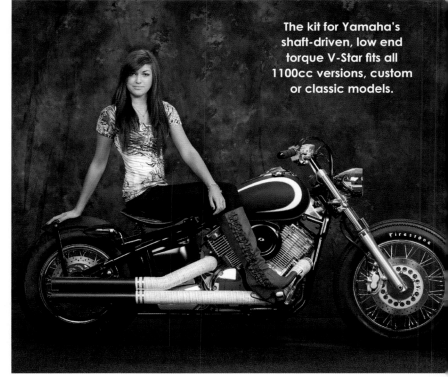

The kit for Yamaha's shaft-driven, low end torque V-Star fits all 1100cc versions, custom or classic models.

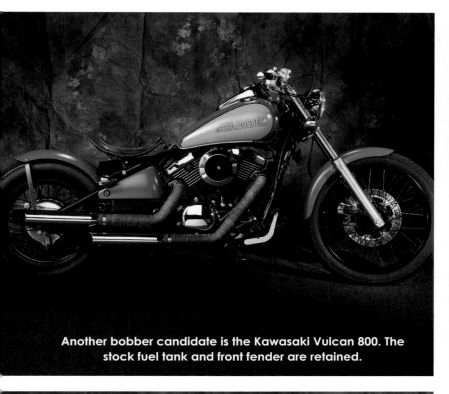

Another bobber candidate is the Kawasaki Vulcan 800. The stock fuel tank and front fender are retained.

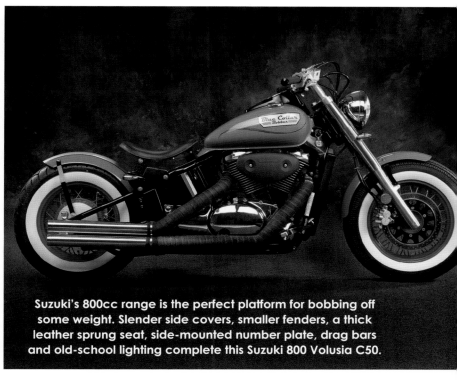

Suzuki's 800cc range is the perfect platform for bobbing off some weight. Slender side covers, smaller fenders, a thick leather sprung seat, side-mounted number plate, drag bars and old-school lighting complete this Suzuki 800 Volusia C50.

The entry-level Suzuki Savage bobber kit fits any S40 models from 1986 onwards. The lightweight machine with its low end torque is ideally suited for riders with a smaller inseam.

Lastly, the Yamaha V-Star 650 kit fits any year or model variation.

Index